AF374032

"I started working with Samantha because I was struggling with conflict resolution and communication in my marriage. Before connecting with Samantha, I had worked with different marriage counselors as well as individual therapy for five years. I still got stuck in negative patterns. Together with Samantha, I have transformed my marriage by learning to identify core issues and focus on personal growth and tools to make lasting change. From the powerful structure of our sessions to the support she provides outside our sessions, Samantha has helped me reconnect with my partner and regain a profound self-love and acceptance. I'm beyond grateful for my GEMMS journey. Thank you, Sam!"

— **Charlotte Kaneko**, Real Estate Investor and Homemaker

"Having worked in various settings alongside Samantha, I can attest to her unparalleled skills as a Marriage Mindshift coach. Her innovative Inner Mosaic method reflects her deep understanding of relationship dynamics while providing practical tools for clients. Samantha is a true leader in the field, inspiring both her clients and her peers."

— **Amanda Youth**, Licensed Clinical Social Worker

"Working with Samantha has changed my life. She helped me change my relationship with myself. I am much happier and more confident. I am driven and focused. While I still face ups and downs, just like everyone else, they don't affect me as much as they did in the past. Things that would have gotten me down on myself seem to roll off my back much easier. Sam has an intuitive way of working, and she asks powerful questions that help you get to the root of how you are feeling. At the same time, her warmth and compassion make you feel very safe and comfortable. She has a knack for helping you bring out the superhero in yourself! I will be forever grateful for the way she has helped me shift my relationship with myself and for the peace and joy that has brought me. Because, ultimately, whether we are starting a business or seeking to improve our relationships with our loved ones, I believe happiness is what we are truly striving for, and that comes from within. Thank you, Sam! This was the most valuable gift I could have gotten!"

— **Bryan Jordan**, Musician and Activist

"Working with my Marriage Mindshift coach, Samantha Kaaua, has been nothing short of transformative. Through her guidance in using her unique Inner Mosaic method, I've learned to lean into my own instincts and trust my judgment when it comes to navigating life's intricate events. Before meeting Samantha, I often found myself relying heavily on what others say and do to make decisions. However, she helped me uncover the power within myself, encouraging me to trust my intuition and unique perspective. Her coaching style isn't about dictating what I should do, but rather empowering me to tap into my inner wisdom. She has taught me to recognize the mosaic of experiences and beliefs that shape my worldview, allowing me to make choices aligned with my true self. Now, I approach life events with a newfound confidence, knowing that I have the ability to assess situations independently. I'm no longer swayed solely by external influences; instead, I trust in my own capabilities to gauge circumstances and make decisions that resonate with my authentic values. I'm immensely grateful for the guidance and encouragement provided by Samantha. Her approach has not only helped me navigate life more confidently but has also unlocked a sense of self-assurance that continues to positively impact every aspect of my life."

— **Rose Barr**, Mindset Coach

"Samantha is not just a regular coach; she is so much more that it is challenging even to put it into words. Samantha's Inner Mosaic modality is beyond a game-changer; it is actually a catalyst of major transformation in someone's life. It helped me understand myself on a very deep level. None of the many modalities I studied before took me to this depth of transformation. It went into my core beliefs, the way I saw myself and the world. I even consider this modality a lifestyle change—you can apply this modality in your daily life: at work, in your business, with friends, with family, and in romantic relationships. Samantha was pivotal during a very challenging moment in my marriage and in my business. I was able to transform my marriage and understand and overcome the personal blocks I had while I was trying to level-up my business. Inner Mosaic was such an incredibly important part of becoming who I am today that I decided to get certified as an Inner Mosaic Coach because I know it can help many other people in this world."

— **Pati Hoyt**, Intuitive Life Coach, Breathwork and
Cacao Facilitator, and Healer

"Working with Samantha has been such a wonderful and life-changing time in my life. Her Inner Mosaic method has helped me to visualize and understand the hidden obstacles affecting my relationship. She has offered amazing tools that have improved my emotional being and helped to transform my marriage and everyday life. Her compassion, knowledge, and special gifts have inspired me to share her teachings with my children. Samantha has made a positive and powerful change in my daily life."

— **Janette M.,** Business Manager

"Talk about 'Aha Moments'! You can feel the emotions change in your mind and body with Samantha's Inner Mosaic method. As an advocate of self-love and a LMFT, I use this tool multiple times a week to support my clients and myself with emotional regulation and internal conflicts. Inner Mosaic is the most effective and unique tool I use to heal the relationship I have with myself and show up authentically with others."

— **Chasidy Wright**, Marriage and Family Therapist
and Self-Love Expert

"Samantha is a gem! As my coach, she played a pivotal role in reshaping my life, guiding me from victimhood to becoming the captain of my own life. Under her mentorship, I've created a life I love. The impact of her Inner Mosaic teachings is evident in the positive transformations I've experienced, particularly in my relationships and in managing 'triggers'—those negative reactions to various situations. As a Certified Inner Mosaic Coach myself, I've incorporated Samantha's teachings into my work with entrepreneur clients, utilizing them as a powerful tool to overcome obstacles and enhance their marketing."

— **Claire Niibu-Akau**, Author, Speaker, and Transformation Biz Coach

"One of the most impactful things I learned being a client of Samantha's was that I could be the change agent in my marriage and relationships. The Inner Mosaic method opened my mind and my heart. I embraced a deeper level of compassion for myself and for those I am in relationship with."

— **Christina Wright-Ah Sam**, Health and Wellness Coach and CEO of Na Alaka'i Hou

"This book is a must-read! It's been my honor and privilege to witness Samantha Kaaua's passion and unwavering commitment to serving women who've decided to stay in their marriages and transform their relationships. It is incredibly empowering for women to know it only takes one person to save their marriage. Samantha walks her talk. She's not only applied these principles in her own life but also has helped hundreds of clients achieve success and live happy, healthy, and long-lasting marriages. Five stars hardly seem sufficient!"

— **Edna A. Castillo**, Best-Selling Author of *Living Your Intuitive Genius*, Transformational Life Coach, Speaker, and Cancer Thriver

"Samantha Kaaua is the real deal. I've followed her journey for the last four years while admiring her navigational prowess. For anyone wanting to transform their relationships this book is a must read!"

— **Mariell Waltner**, Mindset and Success Coach, Professional Speaker, Founder and CEO of MW Solutions

"Samantha's story is all our stories. We've all experienced betrayal, disappointment, and intense pain and have felt overwhelmed by our lives. Life can be hard, relationships can be hard, and learning how to overcome pain can be hard, until we find the right person to help guide us in our healing journey. The truth is, if we want anything of value, we have to be willing to do the hard work. Samantha's done the hard work, and she'll be there for you every step of the way. She's put together a masterful book and created a phenomenal program to help all of us navigate the incredibly difficult times in our lives. She'll totally show you the way to put your life back together more beautifully than you ever thought possible. There is hope, and there is help. Samantha Kaaua's commitment to save as many marriages as possible comes from a pure heart with an incredible amount of experience and diverse training. Do yourself a favor and study this book. You'll walk away with a deeper connection with yourself, and the confidence necessary to create healthy, meaningful, and loving relationships in your life. Be brave, and let the journey begin!"

— **Kathy Biggs**, Senior Transformation Life Coach at Soul Savvy LLC

"Samantha Kaaua is one of the most inspiring people I know. Her personal journey was not easy, but Samantha never gave up, always approaching life with positivity, faith, and the will to go forward no matter what. This strong self-emancipation experience, together with her empathy, intelligence, and professional skills is what I believe makes her an inspiring, transformational coach. I recommend Samantha's book to everyone who needs help and support in their love life."

— **Gordana Radić**, MSc Psychosocial Counsellor and Holistic Therapist

"If I had to pick one word to describe the depths of Samantha Kaaua, it is love. Samantha is one of the most passionate transformational coaches I have had the privilege to work alongside. Her programs and teachings are both heartfelt and courageous. Samantha weaves her expertise into this fantastic book along with her programs. When you connect with Samantha, you can feel her care guiding you while you develop the ability to notice deep-rooted patterns that may be blocking your fullest potential. Samantha will help you unlock your authenticity while wrapping you in the very word that represents her—love."

— **Karie Cassell**, Registered Dietitian, Life Mastery Consultant and Author of the #1 Bestseller *The Domino Diet*

"As Samantha states, this book was 'forged in the crucible of my own marriage.' Let me tell you, as a married man, I know what she's talking about—both the joys and the complications of trying to transform relationships. If anyone can help you rethink your relationship and get you from where you are to the type of relationship you seek, it is Samantha. No, actually it's you. If you make the choice to change you, then you can transform your relationship, and Samantha will show you how."

— **Patrick Snow**, Publishing Coach and International Best-Selling Author of *Creating Your Own Destiny* and *The Affluent Entrepreneur*

"Samantha Kaaua's *Finding Beauty in Your Broken Pieces* isn't just a book—it's an uplifting journey that reimagines relationships through her innovative Inner Mosaic method. With heartfelt storytelling and practical wisdom, Samantha guides us to uncover the beauty within our brokenness, offering a roadmap for healing and celebrating our unique stories. Her work isn't confined to the pages; it's a beacon of empowerment, reminding us that amid life's challenges, our resilience and ability to thrive shine brightest."

— **Candace McKim**, Author of *Yogini's Guide—Intuition Is A Choice* and Founder of the Intuitive Coaching Academy

"In an age when so many marriages end and many seem to choose divorce over the hard work of staying together, Samantha Kaaua offers a counter-culture approach for not only saving but transforming your marriage and other relationships. Her Inner Mosaic method is time-tested to work, not just by her many clients who sing her praises, but through her and her husband's own trial-and-error and finally successful efforts. You will be impressed by Samantha's honesty, you will benefit by her methods, and you will be grateful that *Finding Your Beauty in Broken Pieces* is a book you chose to read."

— **Tyler R. Tichelaar**, PhD and Award-Winning Author of *Narrow Lives* and *The Best Place*

A Counter-Culture Approach

Finding Beauty in Your Broken Pieces

The Art and Science of Transforming Any Relationship

Samantha Kaaua

Finding Beauty in Your Broken Pieces
The Art and Science of Transforming Any Relationship

Copyright © 2024 by Samantha Kaaua. All rights reserved.

Hardcover Published by:
Aviva Publishing
Lake Placid, NY
(518) 523-1320
www.AvivaPubs.com

Softcover and e-book Published by:
Winsome Media Group, LLC
821 W Jordan Oaks Ct
Sandy, UT 84070
(661) 313-7120
www.superbrandpublishing.com

All Rights Reserved. No part of this book may be used or reproduced in any
manner whatsoever without the expressed written permission of the author.

Inner Mosaic® and The GEMMS® are registered trademarks.

Address all inquiries to:
Samantha Kaaua
Samantha@TheGEMMS.com
www.TheGEMMS.com
www.MarriageMindshift.com

ISBN softcover: 979-8-88896-437-8
ISBN ebook: 979-8-88896-425-5

Library of Congress: 2024930170

Editors: Tyler Tichelaar and Larry Alexander, Superior Book Productions
Cover Art: Carlos Acevedo
Hardcover Cover Design and Interior Book Layout: Shiloh Schroeder,
Fusion Creative Works
Softcover Cover Design and Interior Book Layout: Winsome Media Group, LLC
Author Photo: Esther Lambright Patterson

Every attempt has been made to properly source all quotes.

Printed in the United States of America

First Edition

To the little girl or boy who lives inside all of us, who dreams of happy, healthy relationships where they are safe, secure, and loved. May this book allow your voice to be heard and your beauty to be seen. You are more than a dark, jagged, broken piece of glass—you are an essential part of a magnificent mosaic.

I see you; I know you; I am you.

Contents

A Message from Denver

Hi. I'm Denver, Samantha's husband. You're about to read *Finding Beauty in Your Broken Pieces*, a book with real stories of relationships, including mine and my wife's. I'm not one for writing, but it's important for you to know that our journey, with all its highs and lows, is a big part of these pages. We've been through some real challenges, the kind that really test you. It's a story of how we came out stronger, and I think that's something you might relate to.

Watching Samantha write this book has been an eye-opener. I'm not the type to dive deep into emotional stuff, but I can't deny that this book, what she's put into it, has made a difference. It's weird to see our life in print, but if it helps even one person out there, it's all worth it.

We're doing great now, better than I thought possible a few years back. It's been a journey with lots of give and take. The way Samantha looks at things gets to the heart of problems; that's something I'm learning to appreciate more every day.

If you're picking up this book, chances are you're looking for some answers. All I can say is, give it a shot.

You might find something in here that clicks for you, like some of it did for me.

Wishing you the best on your journey,
Denver

Preface

A Note to the Reader

In the intricate dance of human relationships, we often find ourselves amid a tapestry of emotions, mired in patterns that seem inextricably woven from the very core of our being. The title of this book, *Finding Beauty in Your Broken Pieces*, isn't just a phrase but an invocation—a call to those who seek transformation within the heart of their relationships.

As you turn these pages, know that you are holding more than a book; you are stepping into a realm of personal transformation that has been my life's work, and dare I say, my life's mission. Forged in the crucible of my own marriage, which teetered on the brink of dissolution not once but twice, this book is as much a product of my professional insights as it is a testament to personal perseverance. It is my heart's narrative, written during a time when the very foundations of my relationship were being tested and reformed.

The journey of penning these chapters over two years was as arduous as it was enlightening, paralleling the paths many of us tread in the quietude of our lives. I've tailored each word, each method, with the earnest intention that this book serve not only as a beacon of hope, but as a collection of practical tools for those ready to sculpt their raw-edged relationships into something truly magnificent.

The stories I share, both personal and from clients, lift veils to reveal the intimate contours of relationship challenges. To preserve the sanctity and privacy of those who have trusted me with their narratives, I have altered names and personal details—except where permission was granted to keep them unchanged. These stories are not meant to cast shadows of blame or shame but to shine a light on the shared struggles so many couples face in silence.

To all who embark on this journey, I suggest using a companion notebook to chronicle your reflections and progress. The activities laid out are more than exercises; they're milestones marking the path to deeper connection and understanding. While the book can be read in its entirety first, engaging with each activity will, in turn, build the foundation for the next, crafting a cumulative transformation.

Let this book be a safe harbor—a place where the tumultuous seas of relational discord can find calm. My hope is that my Inner Mosaic® method, shared within these pages, becomes not just a well-thumbed reference but a ubiquitous tool in the art of relationship betterment, known and used in households worldwide.

As you embark on this transformative quest, remember: the stories shared, the methods taught, and the lessons learned are all steppingstones to a greater understanding, deeper empathy, and a renewed sense of partnership. Together, let us find the beauty in our broken pieces and, piece by piece, create something whole.

Believing in you,

Introduction

Rude Awakening

I hear the sound of my alarm going off. I jump out of bed with butterflies in my stomach and my thoughts racing a mile a minute. It's 6 a.m. on a beautiful spring morning in 2016. After brushing my teeth and getting dressed, I walk downstairs to gather my things for this life-changing day. I have been preparing for this day for the past two-and-a-half years.

My heart is pounding and my mind spinning, but as nervous as I am, a lightness fills my body knowing I am so close to the finish line. The past two years have been treacherous and challenging to say the least. I gave birth to my third daughter, had a very complicated ablation (awake on the table for eight hours as they shocked me and cauterized fifty-two places in my heart to fix my supraventricular tachycardia), almost lost my grandma to kidney failure, and to top it all off, I am about to graduate with my master's degree in marriage and family therapy.

Today, it will all be over. Eight more hours. That's it. I am about to take my comprehensive exam to determine if I can graduate this summer. All those late nights and long papers are over. I let out a sigh of relief as all the silly stories of grad school life, crazy study sessions, and even crazier client stories pass through my mind.

Focus, Sam. Make sure you bring everything you need for your exam today. I go down the laundry list of items in my head: snacks—*check*, water—*check*, blanket—*check*. *Oh. A cooler.* I search through the cabinets for a small cooler to keep my snacks in during the exam.

I found one. Perfect. As I open it, I realize there's something in it. *Hmm, what's in this black box? I haven't seen this box before.* Looking puzzled, I pick up the box, walk over to the living room where my husband, Denver, is sitting on the couch, and ask, "What is this?"

He looks up. Instantly, his face turns pale. I ask him again, even more confused, "What is this?" His eyes drop to the floor and a flood of tears begins flowing. His body begins to tremble as he puts his hands up to his face.

"Oh, my God! Is this what I think it is?" I ask, angry and disgusted.

Silence. Just silence. I know what it is. It's his weed. But this isn't just recreational weed or medicinal marijuana. It's a symbol of something so much bigger.

This is *ten years* of my husband lying to my face day in and day out about his addiction. This is him choosing to sleep downstairs, telling me the couch is "more comfortable" than our bed. In reality, he wanted to be free to smoke throughout the night. This is him passing out at four o'clock every afternoon and acting grouchy and short-tempered with me and our daughters. This is ten years of lies.

My eyes close as my heart sinks into my stomach. *What's happening right now? What's going on? This is not happening today*, I tell myself in frustration and rage.

I open my eyes and see the terror running through Denver's entire body. He is stuck. Not only mentally and emotionally, but physically stuck. Only six days earlier, he was rushed to the emergency room for a work accident that almost took off his entire foot.

As I glare into his soul, my body begins to tremble, heat rises up from inside me, and I rage, "You are so lucky that you're hurt right now! How dare you? How could you? How could you do this to me? What were you thinking?"

And then a tsunami of emotions hits me. My eyes well up and I burst into tears. My mind is racing in all directions. *How could I be so stupid? There's no way I'm going to pass my exam now. I don't even deserve to be a marriage and family therapist. Look at my relationship—it's a mess. I'm a mess. How am I going to help anyone?*

I sink into the couch next to Denver, totally defeated. The pain in my chest is no longer from my heart condition. This pain is worse. The pain in my chest is the result of being absolutely heartbroken. I feel so betrayed, hurt, and angry.

How did I get here? And where did I go wrong?

My dad once told me, "You always choose the hardest path, but somehow, you always make it work." He wasn't wrong. My path had been winding and rough, but somehow, I always succeeded. But had I finally stretched myself too thin?

My house of cards is finally folding beneath the weight of the world, the weight of all the lies…the lies Denver told me, but mostly, the lies I have told myself all these years.

As a little girl, I swore I would never get divorced. Both sets of my grandparents were divorced before I was born, so I have no recollection of any of them being together. Grandma Toshie was quite bitter about the way Grandpa Roy had treated her. And I never heard Grandma Thelma say anything about Grandpa Joe. Many of my aunties and uncles were divorced too. But my parents' divorce was the most significant for me.

My parents separated before I was one year old. I never knew what life was like with both parents together. The reality is, I only had a few family members who stayed married throughout my childhood. Don't get me wrong; as an adult, I can say I am very grateful my parents separated when they did. But as a little girl, seeing other children who had parents who were together made me want that for myself and my future children.

As I bump up against this sad truth, and face the reality of perpetuating the pattern of divorce in my family, I feel something inside me shift. The promise I had made my young self turned not only into a decision, but a declaration and a burning desire.

I am breaking this pattern!

I didn't know how or what to do to change this unhealthy cycle of broken relationships, but I knew it would certainly end with me. I didn't know if I would stay married or get divorced. However, *if* I did leave my marriage, I was going to leave a whole person. I wouldn't walk away *before* the work was done. And I knew the only "work" I could do was on me.

But where do I start? And what more can I do?

I've been in therapy for a few years now. I've been doing the work on myself. Nothing could have prepared me for the journey I was about to embark on and the beautiful miracles that would come from it.

OVERVIEW

Oh, relationships. They're necessary for the survival of our species, yet their success is so elusive for most of us. A quick Google search on common relationship misconceptions brings up an array of almost laughable results. These misconceptions include everything from the belief that healthy couples never argue to the idea that having a baby will bring you closer together. No wonder we're so confused about how to maintain healthy relationships!

These misconceptions are quite telling. Studies show the majority of marriages end in divorce. That simple fact alone must mean we're entering into relationships with the wrong mindsets.

In the face of poor odds and misconceptions, I am on a mission to help save as many marriages as I possibly can. I believe our world lacks trust and faith; however, if we can restore those, marriages would be more likely to survive the hard times, people would act differently in their relationships, and love would be the guiding light in our world.

In this book, I will share the lessons I've learned in my marriage and through clinical training in the hope that they can help you transform some of your most debilitating limiting beliefs about relationships. Most importantly, I want to empower you to build an even deeper trust within yourself and the world around you so you can become the best version of yourself and completely transform all your relationships.

WHAT THIS BOOK IS NOT

Although I come from a traditional therapy background, I want you to know this book is *not* a therapy book. It's not meant to replace psychotherapy or teach you about therapy in general. I have definitely pulled principles and lessons from the field of psychology, but in no way do I feel I will adequately cover enough ground in this book to exhaust all there is to learn from the field of psychology.

Many people come to me for marriage advice. I will not address classic couples counseling techniques or tools in depth here because I have a somewhat unconventional approach to helping people in their relationships. In fact, I will share an inside secret in these pages about why marriage counseling doesn't always work (and this is coming directly from a former marriage therapist).

This book is also *not* a communication skills book. People often ask me for help in communicating with their partner. They feel so unheard and misunderstood that the only logical solution they can think of is to improve how they communicate. Here's the thing: Yes, improving communication will likely improve your relationship.

However, putting a bandage on a bullet hole without taking out the bullet will only lead to an infection, not healing. Communication is not likely to be the root problem.

Finally, this is *not* a religious relationship book. Many look to religion for support in creating the relationship they want. My references to God or the Universe are in no way tied to a specific religion or religious practice. Instead, I refer to a Higher Power connecting us all together. Some might call this the spiritual side of our nature that we feel in the unseen forces of the world around us.

WHAT THIS BOOK IS

We will explore some counter-culture ways to view and understand relationships. Although some of these principles have been taught for centuries, it's amazing how little our society truly understands them. If they did, we would have much better marriage statistics and much better relationships overall. In other words, the numbers show the majority of people don't understand and can't apply these universal principles to their relationships.

The insights and skills you'll learn here will help you in your relationships, but more importantly, you will gain the power to transform *any* area of your life. For that reason, this is essentially a guidebook to support you in discovering your greatest potential, embracing your gifts, becoming your best self, and shining your light of love in the world.

What makes this book different from other relationship books? Our focus will be on *you*—yes, you. We will not focus on your partner or their behavior. The key to success is to reconnect to your point of power—which is within you. Focusing on your partner's behavior will only continue to leave your power in someone else's hands.

The second reason this book is different from other relationship books is my *lack* of focus on communication skills, boundaries, or intimacy. Most relationship books emphasize understanding your partner's needs, how your partner wants to express or receive love, and working through your relationship challenges together. While these tools are an important part of building relationship skills, this book is focused on the foundation you need to sustain *any* of those practices—it focuses on working on yourself.

Once you learn the skills and tools in this book, you will better understand and be able to overcome relationship challenges. You will walk away with a deeper connection with yourself; a proven, reliable, repeatable process for transforming any relationship; clarity about who you are and what you want; and finally, the confidence you need to have healthy, meaningful, and loving relationships.

Let our journey begin.

Chapter 1

The Triple A's of Transformation

"Beautiful are those whose brokenness gives birth to transformation and wisdom."

— John Mark Green

Every journey begins with a single step, and every story begins with a single decision. For those who seek change, growth, and transformation, this journey often starts with the painful acknowledgment that something is not working, that there are seemingly broken pieces in the beautifully complex mosaic of our lives.

The title, *Finding Beauty in Your Broken Pieces*, points to this book's purpose of learning to see and celebrate each piece of ourselves, even those we see as broken or flawed. Embrace these pieces because they are integral fragments in the stunning mosaic that is each of us. By acknowledging, accepting, and even celebrating these parts, we open a path to inner peace, harmony, and joy, because we no longer resist but embrace our complete self.

Embracing our complete self is *not* a destination, but a continuous journey. It's a journey that requires conscious and dedicated effort and a path that calls for a roadmap. This is where *The Triple A's of Transformation* come into play. The Triple A's of Transformation—Awareness, Alignment, and Action—form the backbone of our transformation process. They serve as our compass while we navigate the intricate mosaic of our lives, leading us toward a deeper understanding of ourselves and our relationships. Let's look briefly at each of the Triple A's to prepare us for our larger discussion of them throughout this book.

AWARENESS

Have you ever had one of those mind-blowing aha moments—a moment when everything suddenly clicks into place, like a 1,000-piece jigsaw puzzle you've been tirelessly working on finally showing you the big picture? That, my dear friend, is the glorious, illuminating power of awareness.

Let me emphasize here that awareness is not an overnight visitor merely skimming the surface of your consciousness. It's the North Star in your journey of transformation, the first A in the Triple A's of Transformation. It's less about fairy-tale epiphanies and more about steadily flipping on the switches in long-darkened rooms, revealing corners of your psyche you've overlooked or ignored for years.

But let's strip away the mystery for a moment: Awareness is not about passively spectating from the sidelines of your life. It's about rolling up your sleeves and really examining your thoughts, emotions, and behaviors, and their effects. It's about shining a spotlight into the dense thicket of your mind, unveiling the deeply rooted patterns and habits that have subtly, but significantly, sculpted your life's path.

Let's not sugarcoat this, though: Awareness, while the first crucial step, doesn't equate to change. It's more like a high-intensity flashlight exposing the mess in a long-neglected room. You can finally see the piles of clutter, but unless you're willing to plunge into the chaos and tidy up, the room will remain a mess. This is the pivotal moment when awareness meets choice—the point where recognizing your reality transforms into the power to change it.

Here's another truth about awareness: It can be challenging, even downright uncomfortable. It brings to light truths we might have dodged or buried deep beneath layers of rationalization and denial. Yet the crux of transformation lies in bravely meeting these truths head-on, accepting them, and using them as catalysts for meaningful change.

Awareness also gives us a wider, more holistic perspective. Our thoughts, feelings, and actions don't operate in a vacuum—they're interconnected with our relationships, environments, and experiences. They're embedded within a vast, complex system extending beyond our personal bubble. Awareness is the wide-angle lens helping us see these complex connections and patterns, revealing the intricate tapestry of our lives.

Cranking up our awareness, therefore, is the pivotal first step on our journey to transformation. It's the wake-up call that rouses us from complacency, opening our minds and hearts to the possibility of change. It's the first layer of fertile soil where we plant the seeds for the next A—alignment.

Let's not forget, though, that awareness is merely the starting line, not the finish. It's the spark that lights the fuse, but without the right alignment and action, the potential for change can fizzle out, leaving us feeling stuck or overwhelmed. That's why we need the remaining A's—alignment and action. These pillars ensure our newfound awareness leads to tangible, meaningful changes that reshape our lives.

In upcoming chapters, we'll delve into the practical tools used to deepen awareness, but for now, think of it as your lantern in the dark. It's that indispensable tool that helps you comprehend where you are, what's happening around and within you, and how you can start paving the path of a transformative journey.

ALIGNMENT

The second A in our Triple A's of Transformation is *alignment*. At first glance, the word "alignment" might evoke images of neatly arranged objects or well-organized plans. But the alignment we're exploring here is far more profound.

Picture a sailing ship leaving a harbor on a clear day. With their destination charted, the captain carefully aligns the ship. Despite being on course, the ship is constantly pushed around by wind and waves. The captain doesn't fixate on these minor changes. Instead, the captain constantly adjusts course, ensuring the ship remains aligned with its destination. This is the dance of alignment—constantly tuning in, adjusting, and realigning amid life's winds and waves.

Think of alignment as tuning your inner radio to the frequency that resonates most authentically with you. It's about harmonizing your thoughts, emotions, actions, and your core values. It's your ability to tap into your highest truth, the essence of your authentic self.

Once you've unlocked the power of awareness, the next crucial step is to align with this newfound understanding—to align yourself with what I refer to as "the Truth with a capital T." Here's where the beauty, and occasionally the beast, of awareness shows its true colors. Awareness is a double-edged sword; it reveals the *reasons* you do what you do, insights that can either propel you forward or weigh you down.

Have moments of introspection left you feeling more depressed than enlightened—have you experienced times when learning more about your patterns and habits spiraled into self-doubt or criticism? If you are nodding, you're not alone. When seen through a lens of self-criticism or depression, every new piece of self-awareness might seem like a new failure. Sentiments like, "Oh great…another thing I've messed up," might echo in your mind, leading you into a self-deprecating rabbit hole.

That's precisely why the step following a bout of awareness is vitally important in guiding yourself toward alignment. It's about harnessing your insights in a positive, empowering way, rather than letting them fuel a cycle of self-defeat.

Alignment practices come in all shapes and sizes. There's no shortage of spiritual texts, teachers, or methods that can help you on this path. Later in this book, I'll share the alignment tools that have helped me personally on my journey. They're practices and mindsets I've found transformative. If you have your own alignment practices, that's fantastic. However, I'd encourage you to try using a beginner's mindset as we delve deeper. There might be new insights waiting for you on this path.

This journey isn't about finding "perfect" balance or reaching a final destination. It's about constantly tuning in, adjusting, and realigning. Just like the ship's captain, you must keep adjusting your course, ensuring you stay true to your journey despite life's inevitable storms.

Just like awareness, alignment isn't a one-and-done deal. It requires nurturing, patience, and continuous practice. But once you've cultivated this skill, it paves the way for the third A—action, bringing your transformative journey full circle.

ACTION

Embracing the final A in our Triple A's of Transformation, we arrive at *action*. If your mind leaps to tireless exertion or endless hurdles, I encourage you to reshape your perspective. Our exploration of action here is not about brute force. It's about guided, purposeful momentum—it's the translation of our awareness and alignment into the material world.

When we speak of action, we often imagine it as something separate from ourselves, as tasks or steps to be completed. However, in our Triple A's of Transformation, action is deeply intertwined with our awareness and alignment. It's an outward manifestation of the internal shifts and transformations occurring within us.

The importance of action cannot be understated. It's the bridge connecting our internal world to the external reality, the conduit through which our dreams, visions, and goals can manifest. You may have experienced moments of profound awareness, or found alignment with your true essence, but without action, those insights would remain locked within you.

Imagine the symphony of a seed transforming into a tree. The seed first absorbs nutrients, aligns itself with the natural forces, then sprouts and grows—each step an action toward its ultimate form. Just as in nature, our transformation requires us to take guided steps, to "sprout and grow" toward our desired state.

So, what prevents us from taking these steps? Often, it's fear or feeling overwhelmed. Fear of failure, rejection, or even fear of success can paralyze us, creating a barrier between us and our desired future. We can be overwhelmed by the enormity of the vision we set for ourselves, making the first step appear monumental.

This is why the concept of "Massive Imperfect Action" (MIA), which we'll delve into deeper later, is vital. MIA encourages us to leap, to embrace the unknown without waiting for perfect conditions. It's about acknowledging perfection isn't the goal—progress is. And progress is achieved step-by-step, action-by-action.

As we move forward in this transformative journey, we need to accept the reality of action—it's neither easy nor instant. It requires dedication, courage, and patience. Yet we learn, grow, and evolve through action. Every step we take, even those leading to setbacks, serves as a lesson, a steppingstone toward our ultimate vision.

Taking action isn't about frantically "doing" but mindfully "being." It's about becoming the best version of ourselves. Each action we take in alignment with our authentic self brings us closer to this ultimate becoming. It adds a tangible form to our dreams and desires, painting the canvas of our life with the vibrant colors of transformation.

Most importantly, remember that the Triple A's of Transformation isn't a one-and-done process. This is more of a wash-rinse-repeat cycle. It's likely once you act, a new awareness will appear and the cycle will begin again. The magic of life and the beauty of transformation is found in this upward spiral of becoming.

As we close the discussion of our Triple A's of Transformation—Awareness, Alignment, and Action— let's hold these principles close. They're not just concepts to understand but values to live by. In every moment of awareness, in every aligned thought, and with each purposeful action, we journey on this path of transformation, creating the life we've always dreamed of.

Part I

AWARENESS

"Awareness is the greatest agent for change."

— Eckhart Tolle

Chapter 2

The Power of Perception

"The reality of life is that your perceptions—right or wrong—influence everything else you do. When you get a proper perspective of your perceptions, you may be surprised how many other things fall into place."

— *Roger Birkman, PhD*

When I finally found my way out of the deep darkness that consumed every aspect of my life for two years after my rude awakening, I saw everything in a whole new light—and I'm not just talking about the world outside. The inner me, the real me, was in a much brighter place too. I started looking back at the journey I'd been on, trying to figure out how I'd made such a massive change in my life. Lots of things played a part in that change, but one thing stood out above everything else—my willingness to look within. Later on in my journey, I came across a book called The Power of Awareness by Neville (pen name of Neville Lancelot Goddard). It wasn't a new book, but it was new to me, and it helped me put into words what I had done to transform through my toughest times.

AWARENESS IN ACTION

In Neville's book, I found a story that felt all too familiar. It was about a woman who completely transformed her relationship with her boss. This is her story, right from Neville's book, along with my thoughts about what I was reading interspersed:

> One day a costume designer described to me her difficulties in working with a prominent theatrical producer. She was convinced that he unjustly criticized and rejected her best work and that often he was deliberately rude and unfair to her. Upon hearing her story, I explained that if she found the other rude and unfair, it was a sure sign that she, herself, was wanting and that it was not the producer, but herself, that was in need of a new attitude.... Her employer was merely bearing witness, telling her by his behavior what her concept of him was.

Wait, what? *She* was the one who needed a new attitude?

Yes. It wasn't my husband who's attitude needed to change; it was mine. This is exactly what I discovered in my marriage. Denver was simply a reflection of the beliefs I had about him, about men, and about marriage.

I suggested that it was quite probable that she was carrying on conversations with him in her mind which were filled with criticism and recriminations. There was no doubt that she was mentally arguing with the producer, for others only echo that which we whisper to them in secret. I asked her if it was not true that she talked to him mentally and if so what those conversations were like. She confessed that every morning on her way to the theatre she told him just what she thought of him in a way she would never have dared address him in person. The intensity and force of her mental arguments with him automatically established his behavior towards her.

Was my private conversations in my head the *real* cause of the way Denver treated me? Was he simply an echo of the stories I was telling myself about him?

These were the powerful questions I asked myself that allowed me to increase my awareness of my part in the problem.

She began to realize that all of us carry on mental conversations, but, unfortunately on most occasions these conversations are argumentative…. When she realized what she had been doing, she agreed to change her attitude and to live this law faithfully by assuming that her job was highly satisfactory and her relationship with her producer was a very happy one. To do this she agreed that before going to sleep at night, on her way to work, and at other intervals during the day she would imagine that he had congratulated her on her fine designs and that she, in return, had thanked him for his praise and kindness. To her great delight she soon discovered for herself that her own attitude was the cause of all that befell her. The behavior of her employer miraculously reversed itself. His attitude, echoing, as it has always done, that which she had assumed, now reflected her changed concept of him. What she did was by the power of her imagination. Her persistent assumption influenced his behavior and determined his attitude toward her.

The primary takeaway here is that the woman in Neville's story didn't wait around for her boss to change his ways; instead, she reshaped her inner perspective, which led to changes in her reality.

Easier said than done. As simple as this sounds—just change the story you're telling yourself and your whole life will change—it certainly isn't easy.

Looking back, as I mentioned earlier, I realized I had done something very similar in my marriage, even though I didn't realize it at the time. Like the woman in the story, I had decided to change my attitude toward Denver. Instead of focusing on the things that made me angry or disappointed, I started focusing on love, understanding, patience, and most of all, gratitude. And you know what? As my outlook changed, so did my husband's behavior. That's the amazing power of perception.

After reading Neville's book and finding a way to put words to my experience, it hit me—my journey out of the darkness had everything to do with the way *I* perceived the world around me.

ESCAPING VICTIMHOOD

Perception is a funny thing. Unless we're aware there are other ways to perceive a situation, we will likely maintain the same point of view. That's exactly why becoming *aware* of other perceptions of my life became the key to moving *through* the darkest night of my soul rather than sitting in it.

I realize now that escaping victimhood wasn't only necessary to save my marriage, but it was necessary to save my life. So many people look through the lens of victimhood without knowing it. Sometimes, the most positive people in our lives still live from a victim mentality. Other, more negative people can never see the good in the world around them.

I have learned from my mentors and teachers that when we perceive everything is happening *to* us, we give away our power to the circumstances, situations, and conditions around us. In this state, our life experiences and emotions are determined by others' thoughts, feelings, and actions. An overwhelming feeling of powerlessness, hopelessness, frustration, and anger can dominate our lives when in this state of mind.

As I moved through my feelings of frustration and anger, it hit me one day that I was sick and tired of being sick and tired. The irony was, I was a substance use counselor at the time, so I heard that saying daily. But I wasn't an addict. Or was I? Was I addicted to feeling sorry for myself? Did I like pointing my finger at everyone around me rather than taking responsibility for my life?

My head would have told me no, but my heart knew better. The reality was that I got some sad satisfaction from being able to throw my hands in the air and say, "It's not *me*. It's not *my* fault." This was a hard one to admit to myself. I had worked on myself for years in therapy, was always enrolled in some sort of self-development program, and prided myself on consistently growing and evolving.

Once I admitted to myself I was living in a state of victimhood and decided I was done living in fear and frustration, I finally reclaimed my power by owning my experiences. Learning about manifestation and other spiritual teachings helped me step into this new perception that life is happening *by* me.

It's such a refreshing feeling to take responsibility for the life we live. That doesn't mean the things that happen to us are our fault. What it means is we have a choice—the *response*-ability—the ability to decide what meaning we give and how we want to respond to any circumstance. And although it can be daunting and depressing at first, when we truly realize the power of this perspective, a whole new world seems to appear. A playground of possibilities opens for us, and a child-like curiosity emerges. The question becomes, now that we're in conscious control of our life experiences: What amazing things can we create in our lives?

Here's the thing—this perception is great as a steppingstone to the next level of life, but we don't want to live here forever. You see, when we take responsibility for all our life experiences without leaving room for a power greater than ourselves, we take the weight of the world on our shoulders. Often, the word responsibility gets mistaken for blame or shame. Although we can own the role we played in creating our life experiences, that's completely different from blaming and shaming ourselves for what's happened.

That's what makes the third new perception that life is happening *through* us so powerful. Rather than being the sole creator of our life experiences, what if we were the co-creators? What if there was a Grand Overall Design or an Infinite Intelligence working with us and through us? Whether you call it God, the Universe, or Divine Power, acknowledging the amazing energy of Life and allowing it to flow *through* us helps us create an even greater life than we could ever imagine.

METACOGNITION

In rounding off the exploration of perception, let's delve into another crucial concept: metacognition, also known as the "observer self." This principle refers to the ability to notice yourself—your thoughts, feelings, and actions. It's akin to stepping out of your body and watching yourself respond in a situation. In personal development circles, this awareness is often referred to as your inner voice.

Metacognition, your ability to notice what your inner voice is saying, is a foundational element in your journey toward awareness and transformation. It's not just another tool; it's a cornerstone upon which you build the rest of your transformation process. If you can discern your attitude, pay attention to your thoughts, or even recognize whether you're operating from a victim or an empowered mindset, you're already making significant strides on the path of transformation.

Remember, this metacognitive ability isn't static—it's a muscle. If you don't exercise it, it will atrophy. So, in the context of your relationships, start noticing the subtleties. Are you keeping score? Are you having a silent, accusatory conversation with your spouse? Are you operating from the disempowering mindset of a victim or the empowering stance of an observer? Cultivating curiosity about your thoughts can provide powerful insights, such as, "Am I blaming and shaming, or am I taking ownership of my part in this situation?"

This metacognitive tool, this mental muscle, will be pivotal in elevating your awareness. However, awareness alone cannot change or transform your life. It's a crucial first step, but it's merely the foundation upon which you build your house of transformation.

Now that you understand the importance of using the power of perception to increase your awareness and move out of victimhood, let's take some time in the following chapters to explore *how* to do it.

Chapter 3

A Perfect Reflection

"The way we experience the world around us is a direct reflection of the world within us."

— Gabrielle Bernstein

We've already learned we first need to use our mental metacognition muscle to become aware of the thoughts we are thinking, the feelings we are feeling, and the actions we've been taking. But what do we do with this awareness, and why is it so important to notice?

Well, let's start by exploring what is known as "The Law of Thinking." This Universal Law says our thoughts cause our feelings, our feelings cause our actions, and our actions cause our results. Therefore, the only way to change our results, including our relationships, is to first understand and become aware of what we've been thinking. Now let's take this one step further. Is there an even deeper *cause* than our thoughts? Yes. In fact, most of our conscious thoughts stem from our subconscious core beliefs.

Okay, so let's recap—if our beliefs form our thoughts and our thoughts are the cause of our results, that means the *true* cause of our results is our *beliefs*. Now this is a game-changer. To change our relationship results, all we need to do is identify and transcend our disempowering beliefs.

But how do you know what beliefs are causing chaos in your relationships? Especially when they're subconscious. Well, the thing about results is they never lie. Your most challenging and most intimate relationships tend to give you insight into your hidden, subconscious beliefs. For many, your most intimate relationship will be with your spouse. For others, it might be with a parent, sibling, child, or even a boss. Technically, all relationships can help you be more aware of your beliefs, but the one you find most challenging will give you the greatest gifts.

Okay, if we want to completely transform our relationship, all we need to do is change our beliefs, right? Yes. And to figure out what beliefs have been holding us back, we can simply look at our spouse or most intimate relationship, correct? Yes. But before we continue, let's take a moment to break down what a belief actually is.

In my understanding, based on years of education and experience in the field of psychology, I have learned beliefs are simply thoughts that have been programmed into our subconscious. When we're babies, we are belief-free. Over time, our parents, family, friends, and society introduce their thoughts (and beliefs). We also witness actions and events that led us to come up with conclusions about life and the world around us.

Through our natural survival instinct to make sense of our experiences, beliefs are formed and then imprinted on our subconscious. Those beliefs are the construct through which we experience life, the lens through which we view the world.

ACTIVITY: IDENTIFYING YOUR CORE BELIEFS

Let's take a moment to see if you can spot some of your beliefs. You were likely brought up on sayings such as "Money doesn't grow on trees" or "You can't trust people." These are just two beliefs you may have about life. What about some of the more positive ones? How about "Everything in life happens for a reason" or "Family first"?

Now it's your turn. Write down ten to twenty common sayings or unspoken "rules" you heard growing up. Don't judge them as good or bad. Just notice them and write them down.

What about relationships, marriage, the opposite gender, or people outside the family? Add another five to ten common sayings you heard growing up about relationships. Again, just notice them and write them down without judgment.

(Pro tip: If you want to take this a step further, using your metacognition, notice the feelings attached to each of your beliefs. Do they bring up negative emotions? Or do you feel empowered and expansive when you hear them? Take extra time to identify how these beliefs influence your feelings.)

Your core beliefs likely lie within this list. You live by some while spending your whole life trying to avoid others. Often, these beliefs may have served you to some degree while growing up; therefore, they were reinforced over time. But now you are no longer a child, dependent on those around you for food, shelter, and safety.

As a result, these beliefs can become limiting and hold you back from having the relationship you would love. Now that you've identified some of your core beliefs, how do you change them—especially if the belief hurts more than helps at this point?

Here's where the power of perception comes into play. You get to choose how you want to perceive your relationships and the people in your life. You have a choice to see them through a victim lens or as part of life happening *through* you.

But don't worry about that just yet. In Part II, where we will talk about the second A in the Triple A's of Transformation: Alignment, I will share my number-one tool for helping shift perspectives to change beliefs.

For now, let's take some time to reflect even further on your most challenging relationship and see if any other beliefs surface.

ACTIVITY: FACING YOUR REFLECTION

What do you find most frustrating about your partner or your most challenging relationship? What are your pet peeves about them? What are the recurring arguments? Irritations? Resentments? Take a moment to journal on these questions. Allow yourself to vent and find the deepest core wound that might have been left by this person or maybe someone else in your past.

Remember, this part of the process can take some time. You will know when you've reached a core belief because it will be reflected in multiple aspects of your life or show up multiple times.

An example of a deep core wound that turned into a core belief and was reflected in my relationships was "Men leave me." As a product of divorced parents, I mostly grew up with my mom. I never knew what life was like with both parents at home, but what I did know was my dad wasn't around for most of my childhood. My parents' divorce played a significant role in my core belief that men leave me.

When I was only seven, a family friend I called Uncle Richard suddenly died. He was a father figure to me when my dad wasn't around. Uncle Richard picked me up from school every day and spoiled me with toys and my favorite snacks. He was a friend of my maternal grandmother, whom I consider my second mom.

Although no one could have predicted he would pass away so suddenly, as a little girl, it felt like he left me. It was yet another man who left. Later, when I started dating, I had two other experiences that reinforced this belief. The first was when some girls at my middle school convinced my "boyfriend" at the time to break up with me. The second happened in high school when my then boyfriend "left me" and became best friends with many of my soccer teammates.

As you can see, this recurring theme left an imprint on my subconscious and created a core belief. This belief was created to keep me safe by keeping my guard up. And although it was formed with the best intentions, it made me a codependent partner, and ultimately, created more and more experiences reinforcing this belief.

Now, it's your turn. Pause for a moment to reflect on the questions I asked above. Give yourself space to journal about the most challenging parts of your relationship.

When I finally accepted the idea that "Your partner is a perfect reflection of your beliefs," a new opportunity arose—the possibility of a new relationship, not just with my husband, but with myself. And so, the journey of building a healthy relationship began.

Chapter 4

A Foundation of Self-Trust

"Self-trust is the first secret of success."

— Ralph Waldo Emerson

A year and a half after my rude awakening moment, Denver told me he was finally ready to try therapy. After his second session, he told me he was using again behind my back and had been for nine months.

At that point, I felt burnt out, frustrated, and overwhelmed. I was working at a substance use treatment center as a counselor and came home to an addict I couldn't seem to help. I also felt like a fraud. I felt hopeless, helpless, and so alone.

I would come home from work early and just lie down on my bed and cry for hours. I was ready to give up. I had no more left in me. All my own therapy, spiritual studies, going to a psychic for answers, leaning into what I learned in grad school about marriages, and learning about addiction at work had brought me to a dead end. I even went to Al-Anon, knowing I was a part of the problem but having no idea what to do anymore. I was so lost and confused, and it seemed like absolutely no one could help me.

But despite feeling lost and confused, I knew one thing for sure: My husband had to earn back my trust. Because that's what I had been taught my whole life: Trust must be earned. And since my husband had lost my trust, he was going to have to earn it back. And *trust* me, I wasn't going to make it easy.

Every day, when Denver came home, I asked him if he had "used" (smoked). Our agreement at the time was he would tell the truth or it would be over between us. (Very rigid thinking, right? Can you relate to this? Does it sound familiar?)

I wanted to punish him. I wanted him to feel my pain. I wanted him to suffer too. But beneath that, I was scared. Scared he would fool me again. Scared I wouldn't see it coming. Scared he would break my heart, or worse, break our daughters' hearts.

Fear took away any trust I had in myself and left me empty and broken. Even the parts of myself I once trusted came into question.

One day, it all came to a head when Denver walked in the door after work and I greeted him with a smile and gratitude that quickly melted into anger and resentment. It was a day like many days before where I wanted to subconsciously punish him for everything he had done.

And then it happened. Denver asked me a life-changing question: "When are you going to start trusting me again?"

My automatic response was, "When you prove you're trustworthy." And, of course, I went on to remind him he had lied to me for ten years, so I didn't know how long it would take.

But then something miraculous happened. I found a new awareness and realized we were doing it all wrong. We were approaching it backward. *He* didn't need to earn my trust back. *I* simply needed to choose whether I wanted to trust him or not. It was simple.

I know what you might be thinking right now. *What? You're telling me you should trust him after what he did to you? He lied! Is he still lying? He doesn't respect you! Why should you trust him?*

Well, let me ask you what happens when you choose not to trust your partner? Here's what your thoughts might sound like: *They never tell me the truth. I know they're hiding something.* And then you begin to look for evidence, right?

Guess what happens when you assume someone is lying? You send out an energetic signal of mistrust and resentment, and when your partner receives your energy, they panic. Yup, that's right. They get scared you're already pissed off. They start feeling like they're walking on eggshells and just waiting for you to lose it *again*.

Then what happens? You, being hyper-sensitive to the sketchy behavior that always comes with the lies, pick up on your partner's "scared" energy and see them walking on eggshells. Then your mind does this: *They're being too nice right now. They must be hiding something? They're only nice when they've done something wrong or when they want something. And why are they acting so scared? Only guilty people act that way. I knew it. What a liar!*

And then *boom*, you're off to the races: "I know you're lying! What are you hiding? Just tell me already and get it over with! We might as well just call it off. I think you should leave! I can't trust you, and you obviously don't want this to get better!"

Can you relate? Well, it might not be exactly what your marriage or relationship looks or sounds like, but I'm guessing you have *a* relationship where you bump up against the same conflict or challenge over and over again.

ACTIVITY: CHECKING YOUR LEVEL OF TRUST

To ensure you can apply this new perspective, let's take a moment to reflect on where trust is lacking in your relationships. Different relationships demand different levels of trust—trusting someone to do their part of a project is much different than trusting someone with your deepest, darkest secrets.

First, I want you to grab a sheet of paper or turn to a blank page in your notebook. Write your name in the center of the page and draw a circle around it, like this:

This is your first level of trust where you keep the things no one knows about you—your deepest insecurities, etc.

Now, identify the people you have shared your darkest secrets with or you call to celebrate your greatest achievements—sometimes, these people know you better than you know yourself, even if you don't feel close to them. Place them on the outer edge of your circle in another circle like this:

Continue adding people and circles until you reach your least intimate relationships, like in the circle below. (You are welcome to use specific names in place of "best friends," but to illustrate, I chose to consolidate some relationships into groups):

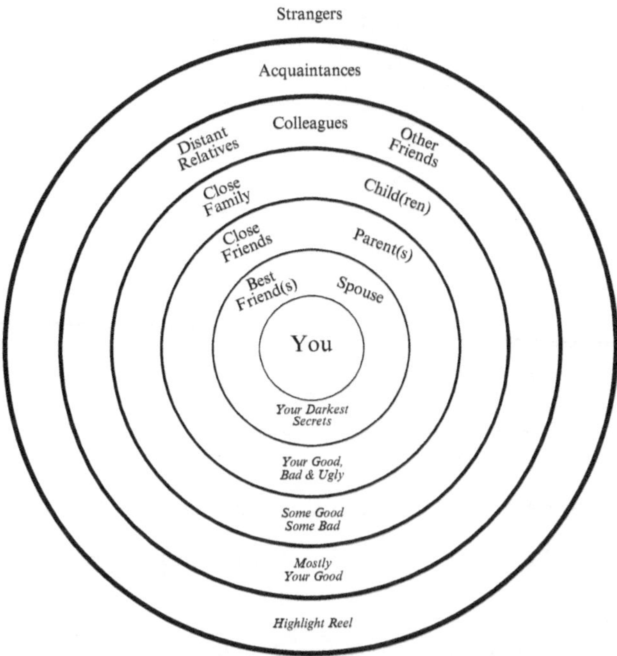

Take some time to reflect on where people are in proximity to you when it comes to how much you trust them. Is your partner or spouse the closest to you? Or is it your friends or a family member? If you have adult children, do they know more about you than your spouse knows? Where would you love everyone to be? Would you want to move anyone closer or further away?

———————————————————————————————

———————————————————————————————

———————————————————————————————

———————————————————————————————

———————————————————————————————

———————————————————————————————

———————————————————————————————

———————————————————————————————

———————————————————————————————

Let me take you back to the moment I realized Denver didn't need to earn my trust—I could simply choose to trust him first.

When I was able to take this apart a little further, I realized it didn't matter whether I trusted my husband. What truly mattered was whether I trusted *myself* to make sound decisions in my relationship, to do the right thing for my family, to be of sound mind and reason, and to navigate any challenge thrown at me at any given moment.

So the question was, "Did I trust myself in my relationship, with my family, to make good decisions?" When I really sat with this question, the answer was a big fat *no*. I didn't trust myself; therefore, I was projecting that onto my husband.

And then it hit me. Of course, I would never trust Denver again—I never trusted him in the first place. And when I dug even deeper, I found I didn't trust myself to be in a healthy relationship, to act like a normal, non-codependent woman. I didn't trust myself to see the warning signs again because I hadn't seen them before.

The even more amazing thing is my lack of self-trust was simply a reflection of my lack of trust in the Universe, God, Infinite Intelligence, the Oneness. I could feel I was part of something greater than me, but I had absolutely no understanding of what that "greater" thing was.

And that's why it's so important to understand all our relationships are built on a foundation of "Self-trust" with a capital S, meaning the part of us that's connected to all things. The part of us that's infinite in nature *and* the expression of a "Higher Self" through the human experience.

One might call this Higher Self God while others simply call it intuition. No matter how we identify with *It*, having a relationship with something greater than our human self and learning how to trust *Its* guidance is important.

ACTIVITY: CONNECTING WITH A HIGHER POWER

Let's take a moment to pause here and check-in with yourself. Do you have a Higher Power? Is it God, Buddha, the Universe, Spirit, Nature, or something else? What is your relationship with this Higher Power? Do you trust that it has your back? Do you believe your life path has been set? Do you feel let down by this so-called Infinite Intelligence? Or do you walk in faith each and every day?

And if say you don't believe in anything, I challenge you to find something. Maybe it's karma or fate? It can even just be science. It's important to believe in something greater than yourself to remove the guilt, shame, and blame you can feel without a greater purpose or path.

We all have room for improvement. We always have an opportunity to deepen our relationship with whichever Higher Power we subscribe to, even if it's simply believing in gravity or the astonishing power of nature.

Where can you grow trust in both your human self *and* your Higher Self? How have you been holding back? Walking in fear? Take as long as you need here because you can't build trust between two people before you've built trust within.

Over the years, the importance of self-love has been heavily hyped. You have probably heard that showing yourself love is the key to happiness. I agree, but I want to add this thought—self-love *is* the ultimate form of Self-trust. And vice versa, Self-trust *is* the ultimate form of self-love.

I know. I know. Love and trust are not one and the same, and neither is self-love or self-trust; however, I argue they are two sides of the same coin. In a healthy relationship, both love and trust are required, but why is it that love can feel like more of our choice while trust can feel like it's completely out of our hands?

This is what causes so much grief and suffering in many relationships—people think they cannot control trust, that the power lies in the other person's hands. This couldn't be more wrong. As I've already said many times, trust is built from the inside out. That's why I said it doesn't matter if we trust the other person; trusting ourselves and the Oneness of the Universe is what counts. And *that* we can control.

All we have to do is learn how to trust *all* parts of ourselves. How do we do that? We'll look at *how* in Part II of this book.

For now, I have a couple of more new insights I want to share to help you access the power of perception and increase your awareness.

Chapter 5

It Only Takes One

"You can change. And you can be an agent of change."

— Laura Dern

I had realized my problem with our marriage lived in me, not in my husband. Denver had his demons, and I had mine. We both needed to work on ourselves. But, ultimately, I had to accept that my husband wasn't the problem.

It was so much easier to point the finger at him, at his addiction, at his deceit, and say he was the problem. But as we learned just two chapters ago, Denver, my husband, was simply a reflection of my own beliefs. That meant the lies, the betrayal, and the addiction all reflected something I believed.

Once I accepted this belief wholeheartedly, I was able to realize all the problems in my life exist *only* within me. And if that's true, the solution to all my problems also exists in me.

But what about relationships? Doesn't society teach us "It takes two to tango" or "Sometimes you just grow apart" or "If they really love you, they will change"? I know that's what I was taught growing up, and in all honesty, those beliefs gave me a codependent mindset. I could write another book about codependency. But for now, let me say codependency does not create healthy, wholesome, and happy relationships.

Back to the point. These common beliefs that say "It takes two people who are willing and actively working together to be in a relationship" or "Love is someone being willing to change *for* you" are actually very disempowering beliefs. Although these beliefs hold an ounce of truth, living by these beliefs will only cause you to feel stuck and powerless in your relationships. You can only move the blame outside yourself when you live by these beliefs. And as I mentioned earlier, your point of power is within you.

Yup, you read that correctly. What I'm encouraging you to do is completely toss away those old limiting beliefs that have been holding our entire planet back from creating and maintaining healthy relationships!

I have seen this time and time again in my own marriage and in many of the relationships I have supported. If you own your problems, you can find your own solutions. Take responsibility for 100 percent of your problems within your marriage and you will begin to see the magic of how *it only takes one person to transform your relationship.*

But let me pull back the curtains a little bit more so you can fully embrace this new awareness and see the power it holds for transforming your life.

THE LAW OF SYSTEMS

When I was studying to become a marriage and family therapist, I was introduced to the concept of systems. This is a fundamental notion within our field, but it may be unfamiliar to many outside it. To put it simply, we believe we exist within a world of dynamic and adaptable open systems influenced by their surroundings. This includes ecosystems and economic systems, but also smaller-scale systems like cities, towns, communities, families, and even our bodies. These systems work together as a whole, adjusting and changing as needed.

Marriages and other relationships are open systems. Open systems strive for homeostasis, a state of balance, harmony, and stability. They seek the path of least resistance, which is precisely what homeostasis embodies.

Understanding this concept is critical because it reveals how change affects systems. For example, in an ecosystem, the extinction of a species requires an adjustment within the whole system. Similarly, in a family, when one member moves away, the dynamics inevitably shift to accommodate the change.

Why? The Law of Open Systems. If you change one part of an open system, the rest of the system must and will adapt to this initial change. This flexibility and adaptability are what make open systems unique. They can grow and change.

This law holds true for individual relationships as well. Two people form an open system. If one person in the relationship changes, the other person, by law, must adjust in response, or the system itself will come to a natural completion.

However, for the system to evolve, the initial change needs to be consistent and steady. Otherwise, the system tends to revert to its original homeostatic state.

Let's look at boiling water as an example. If you put a pot of water on the stove to boil, you must ensure the heat stays on long enough for the water to turn to steam. If you turn the heat off as soon as you see the water moving around in the pot, you will never actually reach the boiling point.

It's the same for relationships. If we're not consistent and steady with our personal changes, they will never take our relationships where we want them to go.

In my own journey, as much as I knew I had to focus on myself and change my own thoughts, feelings, and actions, it was so much easier to fall back on my old ways of blaming my husband for his addiction and lies. And whenever I did that, I was turning off the heat and letting the water cool down. Over time, I learned being consistent mattered, and only after learning how to be consistent with my own changes did I begin to see changes in Denver.

WHY MARRIAGE COUNSELING DOESN'T ALWAYS WORK

As promised, I want to take a moment to explain why marriage counseling doesn't always work and didn't work for me and Denver.

Around the same time I had the epiphany that Denver was simply reflecting my lack of trust in myself, we started seeing a marriage therapist. Denver's therapist referred us to one of the best couples counselors in our area, and I was thrilled to get started.

When we started marriage counseling, Denver had been living at his friend's house for about a month. I had asked him to leave because he wasn't getting better (or trying to quit), and I was slowly but surely losing my mind. We needed space. So, these sessions were the only time we saw each other during the week.

The sessions were great at first. They gave us the space to talk about our feelings and discuss hard topics. Being in the field of marriage and family therapy, I was very mindful that Denver could feel ganged up on, so most of the time, I chose to take a backseat in our sessions and kept pretty quiet.

After attending marriage counseling for a few months, we were starting to hold hands and go out to eat after our therapy sessions. Things felt like they were getting better. And then it happened.

We came in for our weekly session after having a really good week and had little to process regarding our disagreements or frustrations with one another. I didn't want to *waste* our session, so I started to open up about some of my deeper frustrations in our marriage. That's when it all fell apart. Our therapist took *my* side. She asked Denver questions that implied she agreed with me, and he completely shut down. He felt attacked and ganged up on.

I could feel the tension in the room. I knew Denver wanted to get out of there—and we couldn't have gotten out of there any quicker once our session was over. I basically had to chase him down the hall to the parking lot. He was pissed. As we got to our cars, he practically yelled, "I'm never going back to her again." And I knew, right then, if I insisted and took her side, our marriage could be over.

I agreed with Denver—we would never go back to her again. And we have never been back to another marriage therapist since.

Okay, don't get me wrong. I'm not saying marriage therapy is bad. Remember, I was a marriage therapist who saw couples and who helped many of them overcome major challenges. However, what I did learn from my experience is traditional marriage counseling may not always be the best solution for relationship challenges. Often, couples counseling focuses on changing both parties simultaneously, disrupting the homeostasis of the open system without allowing enough time for the system to adapt naturally.

Moreover, some people might find themselves pressured into attending therapy by their partner. That can lead to them feeling defensive during sessions, potentially exacerbating the issues instead of resolving them. That's why couples counseling might not always be the best solution, or could even be counterproductive in certain circumstances, like in my own marriage.

I had given Denver an ultimatum. He wasn't allowed to move back in until we went to couples counseling. That's why he went. Not because he actually wanted to go. The reality is he didn't even want to go to individual therapy. Even though he initiated it, he wasn't ready or willing to take a deeper look at his demons.

While it may seem counterintuitive, focusing on self-change within the system—instead of unnaturally forcing change on all the system's parts simultaneously—can lead to more lasting transformation. Here is where the power of an open system truly shines. As the change agent in your relationship, if you hold on to your transformed state long enough, your partner has the opportunity to rise to the occasion, creating a new homeostatic state in your relationship.

As we continue to explore the role of open systems in our relationships, it's important to understand the central role you play. You're not merely a participant, but a powerful agent of change within the system.

Chapter 6

Everything Is a Relationship

"Relationships are all there is. Everything in the universe only exists because it is in relationship to everything else. Nothing exists in isolation."

— *Margaret J. Wheatley*

I invite you to embrace one more fundamental belief on the journey of transforming your relationships. For some, it may be a familiar idea—for others, a new perspective. Regardless of where you stand, recognizing its importance will serve as the cornerstone for the next phase of our work together.

This belief casts a wide net, encompassing all aspects of your life. It's the understanding that everything we've been exploring together applies universally. And when I say *everything*, I truly mean it. Every relationship, every interaction, every connection you have—be it with a person, an object, or even a thought—all can be navigated using these principles.

We've touched on the concept of open systems and understanding how each part is intricately connected to the whole. From family to strangers passing by, everything and everyone is in constant relation with one another. Sure, we may not label every fleeting interaction as a relationship, but when we think about it, aren't we always in relation to those around us?

This relationship extends even further. Consider the inanimate objects in your life, your surroundings, the environment, the weather. Don't you have a unique connection with these too? An affinity for the cold or a fondness for a cozy armchair—aren't these relationships in their own right? I invite you to broaden your perspective and see the relational dynamics at play in all these aspects of life.

But there's more. As you read these words, you might find your thoughts drifting toward your next meal or an upcoming trip, or maybe you're preoccupied with an ongoing relationship issue. This internal dialogue is also a relationship—a conversation with yourself. You might recognize different "voices" in your head, a variety of personas, each with their own perspective.

This isn't a sign of madness; it's perfectly normal. We all have these inner parts. These aren't distinct entities but parts of our whole self, each with its own relationship to us. They all make up who we are. (I will get into this more later in the book.)

The understanding that you are in constant relationship with every part of yourself, as well as everything around you, is what this belief is all about. The essence of this belief is: *Everything is a relationship*. We relate to everything inside and outside of us. And with that in mind, let's take a look at the different types of relationships we have that we may or may not have considered before.

BODY AND HEALTH

Your body. Your health. What comes to mind when you read these words? Maybe you think of how you look in the mirror or how you feel when you wake up in the morning. Maybe you think of a doctor's visit or your last workout. Now consider this—each of these thoughts and feelings is a part of your relationship with your body and health.

I'm not a physician, nutritionist, or fitness guru. I'm a relationship coach. My job isn't to tell you what to eat or how to exercise, but to help you understand how you relate to your body and health.

Think about how you talk to and about your body. Is it with respect and admiration or with criticism and judgment? Are you grateful for its strength and resilience, or do you often wish it was different?

What about how your body talks to *you*? Do you have any ailments or chronic pain? Did you know these are messages from your body telling you something is out of alignment? Often, people mistakenly feel their aches and pains are something to get rid of, maybe labeling them bad or annoying. But pain is a message waiting to be decoded. I often ask my clients to look out for sensations or shifts in their body while discussing certain topics. It could be butterflies in your stomach, tension in your chest or shoulders, or even a ball in your throat. Allowing your body to have its voice can help you get out of your head and listen to your heart's deepest desires.

Similarly, your relationship with your health isn't just about your medical records. It's about how you perceive your wellbeing, how you respond to sickness, and how you prioritize health in your daily life. It's about how you navigate stress, harmonize work and rest, and make choices that either nourish or deplete your vitality.

Remember, your body isn't just a vehicle for your mind and spirit. It's an integral part of you, deserving of love, care, and attention. Your health, similarly, isn't a commodity but a dynamic, living part of your experience. Just as in any relationship, nurturing the bond with your body and health requires respect, understanding, patience, and constant effort.

In life's journey, it's crucial to foster a loving, compassionate, and respectful relationship with your body and health. After all, they're with you every step of the way, supporting you in every endeavor. The question is: How will you choose to relate to them?

CAREER AND LIFE PURPOSE

Moving forward, let's consider your career or life purpose. Can you really have a relationship with your career and with life purpose? Absolutely! You relate to everything around you, and your career and life purpose are no exceptions.

Your career isn't just a means to an end. It's not merely a source of income or a way to pass the time. It's a significant part of your life and shapes your daily routine, influences your personal growth, and adds to or subtracts from your sense of fulfillment. Your relationship with your career reflects how you perceive and feel about your work, and how it harmonizes with other aspects of your life.

Similarly, your life purpose isn't just a grand, elusive goal out in the distance. It's an intimate part of your being and influences your decisions, shapes your values, and fuels your passions. Your relationship with your life purpose reflects how you interpret your experiences, how you pursue your goals, and how you make sense of your place in the world.

Both your career and life purpose shape your identity, contribute to your sense of self-worth, and influence how you interact with the world. However, that doesn't mean they're static or unchanging. Just like any relationship— the bond you share with your career and life purpose can evolve, transform, and even be completely reborn as you grow and change.

Recognize the dynamic nature of these relationships. Learn to navigate their ebbs and flows. And remember, it's not just about what your career and life purpose can give you, but also what you can bring to them—your unique talents, your passion, and your dedication. After all, it's in this mutual exchange, this dance of giving and receiving, that relationships truly come to life.

So, as you walk this journey, take a moment to reflect on your relationships with your career and life purpose. How do you relate to them? And most importantly, how can you nurture these relationships to serve you and the world better?

TIME

Shifting our attention to another important aspect of our lives, let's consider time. Yes, you read that right. Time. While it may seem abstract, you indeed have a relationship with time.

Consider your daily life. Are you always racing against the clock, feeling like there's never enough time in the day? Or perhaps you view time as an ally, something you can work with to achieve your goals and ambitions? The way you perceive, value, and use your time speaks volumes about your relationship with it.

Time is a unique element in our lives; it's the one resource we all have an equal amount of each day, yet how we choose to spend it varies vastly from person to person. It's not just about managing time efficiently; it's also about understanding its value, respecting its limitations, and recognizing its potential.

Time, like other relationships, requires harmony. It's easy to fall into the trap of becoming overly busy, packing our schedules so tightly we leave no room for rest, reflection, or spontaneous joy. On the other hand, underusing time, letting it slip away without purpose or focus, can also lead to dissatisfaction. The challenge lies in finding harmony, in a way that respects both our goals and our need to relax and enjoy life.

Moreover, your relationship with time is also about how you perceive the past, present, and future. Do you often dwell on the past, or do you constantly worry about the future? Or do you make a conscious effort to live in the present, embracing each moment as it comes?

Your relationship with time isn't fixed; it can change and grow. Recognizing and adjusting unhealthy patterns in this relationship can reduce stress, increase satisfaction, and give you a greater sense of control. Remember, time is a precious commodity, and how you choose to interact with it fundamentally shapes your experiences.

MONEY

Now, let's venture into an often complex and emotionally charged topic: your relationship with money. Have you ever paused to consider what money means to you? What emotions arise when you think about it? Do you have feelings of abundance, security, and freedom? Or stress, scarcity, and constraint? Your emotional response is a powerful indication of your relationship with money.

In our society, money is often linked to our sense of self-worth and achievement. It's viewed as a measure of success, leading to feelings of inadequacy or dissatisfaction if we perceive we don't have enough. Remember, money is more than just a medium of exchange—it's a form of energy. Its value is determined by the meaning and power we ascribe to it.

The word "currency" implies a current—a flow of energy. Shifting our perspective to see money as a dynamic energy exchange rather than a static object can transform our relationship with it. If we approach money with fear or anxiety, it can skew decision-making, obstructing our capacity to save, invest, or enjoy the life-enhancing experiences money can provide.

It's worth noting that money issues are often the hidden third party in marriages and relationships; they can cause a breakdown of trust, communication, and even love. Money isn't just energy—it's a silent partner in our relationship system, capable of creating tension, mistrust, and resentment if not respected as such.

When we view money as a part of our relationship system, it becomes clear it has its own dynamic within that system. Each person in the relationship relates to money differently based on their upbringing, experiences, beliefs, and values. One might be a saver, considering every expense and finding comfort in growing their savings. The other might be a spender, finding joy in the experience and the here-and-now, seeing money as a tool for enjoying life.

This micro system of how each partner relates to money can often lead to challenges. When two differing perspectives collide, it's common for misunderstandings, disagreements, and tension to arise. For example, the saver might view the spender's behavior as careless or irresponsible, leading to feelings of anxiety or resentment. On the other hand, the spender might feel constrained, controlled, or judged by the saver, leading to feelings of guilt or defensiveness.

It's crucial to remember that neither relationship with money is inherently right or wrong. They're simply different, shaped by individual experiences and beliefs. Understanding and respecting these differences is the first step toward harmony. Open, honest communication about how each person relates to money and why can help bridge these differences. That doesn't mean one person has to adopt the other's relationship. It's about finding a middle ground that respects both perspectives.

Establishing a relationship with money based on respect, gratitude, and open communication can invite a flow of opportunities and create harmony. Suppose we saw money as flowing energy within our relationships. How would this alter our conversations about it? How would we treat it differently? Changing our perspective from scarcity to abundance can shift our financial reality, enhancing not only our intimate relationships but also our overall life experience.

Deepening our understanding of our relationship with money and investing time and energy into cultivating a healthier relationship with currency can enhance our overall life quality. Recognizing everything, including money, is a relationship to be nurtured and respected is the key to leading an abundant and fulfilling life.

ENVIRONMENT

Our environment, the space we inhabit and interact with every day, plays a significant role in our lives. Its influence is often subtle, but it shapes our experiences, our moods, and our overall sense of wellbeing.

Think about your relationship with your home. Does it invite relaxation and creativity, or is it cluttered and chaotic, evoking stress? Our homes are more than just physical shelters; they're spaces holding our emotions, memories, and dreams. We cultivate a relationship with our environment that supports our wellbeing and reflects our inner state by making conscious decisions about what we bring into our homes, how we organize them, and how we maintain them.

Similarly, consider your relationship with the broader environment: your neighborhood, city, country, and ultimately, the planet. We are inherently interconnected with the natural world, and how we interact with it affects not only our personal wellbeing but also the health of our planet.

Do you enjoy spending time in nature? How do you feel when you walk through a park or along a beach? These interactions are aspects of your relationship with the natural environment. They're opportunities for nourishment, reflection, and connection.

Furthermore, our actions, big or small, matter. The choices we make—such as recycling, conserving water, or using public transportation—reflect our relationship with the environment. These choices matter, and they contribute to a sustainable future.

At the heart of our relationship with our environment is the realization that it's not separate from us. It's an integral part of our lives, and we are a part of it. Our relationship with our environment is, therefore, a relationship with ourselves. By nurturing this relationship, we create spaces that support our health and happiness, and we contribute to the wellbeing of our planet.

UNIVERSE OR SPIRIT

When we talk about our relationships, we often limit our discussion to people and tangible things. But what about our relationship with the intangible, the spiritual, or, as some may refer to it, the Universe or God?

Your relationship with the Universe or Spirit is a deeply personal and often profound part of your life. Some people might define this relationship through the lens of religion, while others may see it in more secular or philosophical terms. Whatever form it takes, this relationship can offer a sense of purpose, provide comfort in times of trouble, and inspire awe and wonder.

Recognize that this spiritual relationship is an ongoing dialogue, not a monologue. It's about listening as much as it's about asking or expressing. Whether we're walking in nature and feeling the grandeur of the galaxy, meditating in silence, or finding solace in a religious ritual, we are engaged in a dialogue with the Universe or Spirit. They're opportunities to relate to something larger than ourselves.

Your relationship with the Universe or Spirit is also about trust and surrender. Trust in the grand scheme of things, and surrender control over outcomes. Understand that we're not alone, and a force, an energy, a spirit connects us all.

This relationship, like any other, requires nurturing. Regular spiritual practices, mindfulness, reflection, and acts of kindness can all enrich this connection. The beauty is, there are no set rules here. This is your personal relationship, and it's up to you to discover, explore, and cultivate it in a way that resonates with you.

Acknowledging and nurturing your relationship with the Universe or Spirit can bring a deeper sense of connection and meaning. It can be a source of guidance, strength, and peace as you navigate your journey.

This relationship can also remind us of our interconnectedness, not only with the people around us but with the universe as a whole. We'll discuss this in greater depth in Chapter 10: Metaphysics and Mental Science.

INTEGRATING AND NURTURING ALL RELATIONSHIPS

Having explored the diverse array of relationships that comprise our lives—from our body and health to our career and life purpose, from our understanding of time and money to our interaction with our environment and even our connection to the Universe or Spirit—it's time to take a step back. It's time to examine how these relationships are interconnected, how they influence one another, and how they collectively shape our lives. After all, we're not just in a relationship with one aspect of our life; we're in a relationship with everything, both inside and around us.

Consider a painter's palette. The artist doesn't use just one color but skillfully blends various hues to create a masterpiece. Similarly, we must learn to integrate and nurture all our relationships. This is a deliberate and thoughtful process. It means acknowledging each relationship, understanding its significance, and striving to create harmony with and between it and all the others.

Remember, each relationship has its unique characteristics, demands, and rewards. Our relationship with our health is different from our relationship with money, just as our relationship with time differs from our relationship with our environment. Understanding these distinctions is the key to fostering healthier, more fruitful relationships across all aspects of our lives.

At the same time, it's vital to remember that nurturing these relationships isn't a one-time event but an ongoing process. It involves constant adjustment, continuous learning, and frequent self-reflection. It's about maintaining harmony in this complex web of relationships that forms the tapestry of our lives.

In the next part of the book, we will use these principles to dive deeper into the *alignment* phase of the Triple A's of Transformation process. Using my Inner Mosaic method, we'll delve into a new dimension of self-understanding and growth. We'll learn to align ourselves, our thoughts, feelings, and actions, in harmony with all our relationships. Because true and lasting transformation doesn't happen in isolation—it happens when all the pieces of our life's mosaic come together in beautiful synchrony. Get ready for a fascinating journey into the heart of Alignment.

PART II

ALIGNMENT

*"When you align with your true self, you
open the door to infinite possibility."*

— Debbie Ford

Chapter 7

The Inner Mosaic Method

"She never seemed shattered; to me, she was a breathtaking mosaic of the battles she's won."

— Matt Baker

We have many different parts within ourselves, and whether we know it or not, we have a relationship with each of these parts.

I have some good news for you. In the next few chapters, we will learn what these parts are, how they function in our lives, and how to build relationships with these parts of ourselves to help dissolve any blocks and overcome any obstacles.

THE INNER MOSAIC

Just like mosaic artwork, we are made up of unique parts or pieces that, when put together, create a beautiful whole image. Until we become familiar with all the unique parts or pieces within us, we won't be able to truly bring all the pieces together to create the whole image. In essence, once we learn to love and accept all parts of ourselves, we can access the power of our whole being.

Inner Mosaic is my number-one tool to help clients learn to love and trust themselves fully. And as you learned in the second new belief I shared, *your relationships must be built on a foundation of Self-trust.* Therefore, learning to love and trust yourself is the key to transforming any relationship.

Let me take a moment to talk about how Inner Mosaic was born.

While in graduate school, I learned four systemic models I really resonated with: 1) Bowenian, 2) Attachment 3) Emotionally Focused Couples Therapy, and 4) Internal Family Systems. Other models such as Solution-Focused Brief Therapy and Narrative Therapy have also influenced me. However, the first four were the inspiration for what I now call Inner Mosaic.

Let me briefly break down these formal systemic therapeutic models to show you how I came up with mine. I'll use some therapy talk in here, but hang with me.

The Bowenian model was created by psychiatrist Murray Bowen. I originally loved his model because he looked at family history and identified patterns. Bowen came from a psychiatry background where the goal was mostly to find dysfunction. And, dare I say, *all* therapists enter this field to first and foremost make sense of and change their own dysfunctional patterns. That's why I enjoyed this model early on in my studies. I later moved forward from this model, knowing continuing to only focus on the past wouldn't help me truly create the transformation I was longing for. However, I still see the benefit of briefly looking back to find any patterns that can give us clues about subconscious beliefs that could be silently holding us back. That's why it still influenced the development of the Inner Mosaic model.

Attachment Theory was originally created by John Bowlby and Mary Ainsworth. They stressed the importance of a child's emotional bond with their caregiver and how that influences all of the child's future relationships. This model helped me to understand the foundation of inner child work.

Another very influential model under the umbrella of Attachment is Sue Johnson and Les Greenberg's Emotionally Focused Couples Therapy (EFT). Their model of how couples interact and communicate based on their original attachment styles has been highly influential in my work.

Internal Family Systems (IFS), created by Richard Schwartz, is a model I learned about toward the end of my graduate program. IFS proposes different parts of the self exist within a person. This model identifies three major parts: exiles, firefighters, and managers. As you can tell from the name, exiles are the parts of yourself you shove away into a closet to hide from the world. The firefighters are the parts that do damage control once things go wrong. And the managers try to keep everything and everyone together. What I loved most about this model was simply that it acknowledges each of us has different parts making up our whole self. I started to move away from the model when it came to labeling exiles, firefighters, and managers. I learned putting a label on someone or a part of someone can cause them to get stuck because we box them into a certain personality trait. In fact, all the parts of self are dynamic and have a range of emotions.

These four models and many others were the incubators for my own model of coaching.

THE SHIFT FROM THERAPY TO COACHING

After working as a counselor and therapist for a few years, I realized I didn't want only to become *aware* of how my past was playing out in my present, but I wanted to *do* something about it. I wanted to use my awareness to change my present experience.

Here is where the influence of Solution-Focused Brief Therapy, created by Steve de Shazer and Insoo Kim Berg, came into play and influenced the Inner Mosaic model. I honestly think the coaching field was born from the solution-focused brief therapy model. Awareness of the past can only support you if you use it to do something different in the present. And that's exactly what I wanted for myself and all my clients—I wanted a way to use self-awareness in the here and now.

Narrative Therapy, developed by Michael White and David Epston, was one of my least favorite models while I was in school along with Solution-Focused Brief Therapy. But over time, as my desire for change and transformation overshadowed my need to understand my past, I really grew to love the concept of changing the narrative or story we are telling ourselves about any given situation. This is how Narrative Therapy influenced my Inner Mosaic model.

Here's how the Inner Mosaic method works. When you bump up against a problem, and I can stretch to say any problem or challenge, the Inner Mosaic method helps you increase *awareness*, *align* with your highest and most divine self, and take *action* from this place of alignment.

In short, it allows you to pause long enough to make a conscious decision about how you want to present yourself in the moment. And it allows you to regain your personal power in determining how you want to respond to the world instead of letting your circumstances, situation, or condition dictate how you think, feel, and act.

When I first started this work, I actually called it Shadow Work. I realized later many people already used the name Shadow Work because in reality, many people run away from their shadow—the parts of themselves they don't want the world to see, the parts they don't want to acknowledge.

I originally got the name Shadow Work from a comic strip I once saw. It was of a man running away from his shadow. As the man ran farther away, the shadow grew bigger and bigger until it looked like this big scary monster chasing him. But then the man stopped. He decided to turn toward his shadow instead. As the man walked closer and closer to his shadow, it began to shrink. The second to last image of the comic strip was of the man holding his tiny shadow in the palm of his hand, and the very last image was of the man hugging his shadow.

This comic strip was a very important life lesson for me and everyone I've helped through this process. The premise of this technique is to befriend your fears. When you embrace the parts of yourself that look scary, you can bring them down to size so they don't look like a big scary monster chasing you. And like your shadow, you can't run away from your fears, no matter how hard you try. The only way to get rid of your shadow is to shine the light of awareness on it, and that's exactly what we will learn to do in the next few chapters.

MY AHA MOMENT

Before I discovered the true power of the Inner Mosaic, I felt like a crazy person. I was normal at work and with friends, but when I was at home, I became this angry, short-tempered, resentful, spiteful, bitter, grouchy, and irritable monster.

It was a horrible feeling, but I couldn't help it. I didn't want to be that way with my daughters—I only wanted to act that way toward my husband. But I couldn't turn it off at home. That's when I realized when I got home every day, a different part of me (in other words, a different persona) would take over.

Remember my trust issues with the men in my life? Well, through my own Inner Mosaic work, I realized the personas that came out when I was feeling insecure and afraid my marriage was falling apart were seven-year-old Sam Sam and fifteen-year-old Heartbroken Sam. These were the parts of me that had been hurt by men. My insecurity was also reinforced by my parents splitting before I was one and hardly seeing my dad while I was growing up.

When I started looking at my situation through the lens of my Inner Mosaic parts, it all started to make more sense. When I got home from work every day, Sam Sam and Heartbroken Sam took over. A seven-year-old and fifteen-year-old me took charge. And they didn't trust men at all. So the moment they saw Denver, who broke my heart by lying to me for ten years, they wanted to punish him. They pouted and threw tantrums to make sure he didn't do anything like that again.

When I looked at the situation that way, I could give myself a little grace. I knew I couldn't expect myself to act like an adult in those moments because the seven-year-old and the fifteen-year-old me were being triggered. That's when I realized I needed to support my younger selves through the situation, comfort them, and reassure them everything was going to be okay.

It's time to stop telling you how this all works. I want to *show* you and allow you to actually experience this amazing Inner Mosaic process for yourself. In the next chapter, you'll see how this process helps my clients break through their biggest barriers.

Chapter 8

Your Greatest Awareness and Alignment Tool

"The process of becoming unstuck requires tremendous bravery, because basically we are completely changing our way of perceiving reality."

— Pema Chodron

Now that I've taken you through the origins of the Inner Mosaic method, I want to walk you through how to use it to transform your life. You'll also learn what to do when you feel blocked or stuck. Just remember the process requires practice, so don't be discouraged if it doesn't transform you overnight.

STEP 1: IDENTIFY THE SITUATION

The first step to the Inner Mosaic method is to look at the current situation in which you feel stuck.

What's happening or what happened?

Think about the situation you're experiencing right now. This is an important step in the process. Many people learn how to live their lives backward. They look at their circumstances to determine how they should think, feel, and act. Remember earlier when I talked about the Law of Thinking? Well, here's the thing—if we keep looking at our conditions to tell us what to think, feel, and how to act, we end up going in circles as if we were on a never-ending carousel.

That's what I call the cycle of insanity. If you let your circumstances dictate your thoughts, feelings, and actions, you will simply keep creating the same results. But if you learn how to choose your own thoughts *despite* your situation, you will experience your true power— your ability to think your own thoughts and create the results you want. Although you don't want to allow the situation to dictate what you think and feel, it's important to identify the content of the situation so you can avoid getting stuck on it.

ACTIVITY: IDENTIFYING THE SITUATION

Take some time to identify an area in which you feel stuck or challenged in your relationship. What was your most recent argument with this person about? What happened? Who was involved? Was this the first time this challenge came up? Or was this something you've discussed before? What happened before and after your disagreement or challenge with this person? Think of as many details as possible. If you can, remain neutral and try to describe the situation using metacognition, your observer self.

STEP 2: IDENTIFY THE STORY OR THEME

The next step is to identify the story you're telling yourself about the current situation. Another way of looking at this is to identify the theme of what's happening. For example, some themes might be powerless, unprotected, bullied, not good enough, etc.

What story are you telling yourself about the current situation?

The story you tell yourself is how you create meaning in your life. Through the power of storytelling, you can make sense of a situation, and it even helps you to recall events so you can continue to survive, grow, and adapt.

I used to think I was a bad storyteller. I always messed up the punchline to a joke or forgot key parts of a story I was telling. However, as I began to study Universal Laws, I realized stories are the foundation our entire reality is built upon. So, if any part of you feels you're a bad storyteller, I challenge that idea. You have told yourself stories from the time you were a child and could first form your own thoughts. It's simply a matter of learning how to tell stories you love rather than use your storytelling skills to terrorize yourself and create unwanted results.

Take your time through this process. Identifying the story you're telling yourself about the situation will make the next steps a lot easier.

ACTIVITY: IDENTIFYING THE STORY

In the previous activity, you identified the content of the situation you're currently feeling challenged by. It's time to capture the theme or story connected to what happened. Take some time to write about the situation in your journal and find the story you're telling yourself.

Another way to help find the story is to look for patterns or themes in your life. Is there something familiar about the current circumstance? Is it a recurring pattern? The pattern you notice just might be the story you're telling yourself. Write down your story in the space provided below or in a separate journal.

____

____

____

____

____

____

____

____

____

____

____

____

____

____

____

____

STEP 3: IDENTIFY THE PART OF YOU THAT'S SHOWING UP

The third step is to find the earliest memory you have of the theme or story you identified. For example, if you're experiencing a feeling of powerlessness, think about the earliest memory you have of feeling powerless. Make sure you're not straining or struggling but just recalling the earliest memory that pops into your mind when you think of the theme or story. It doesn't have to be the very first memory. Just the earliest memory you can think of. And the younger you were the better. But know that your current conditions and your childhood memory can be two completely different situations with a similar theme or story.

What is the earliest memory you have of the theme or story you're telling yourself about the current situation?

This might look somewhat like inner child work. And in some ways it is. We are looking back to find a time when you experienced similar feelings to your current situation. Often, people are triggered by certain situations that remind them of a traumatic event from their childhood. They may revert to the age they were when the initial incident happened. So, in essence, when a situation reminds someone of a past event, they sometimes take on thoughts, feelings, and behavior as if they were back to the age they were during the original event. We'll talk more about this in a little bit.

It's important to note some of my clients get stuck on this step. They can't connect to the original event for a few reasons. The first reason being the moment was so traumatic they blocked it out of their consciousness. I normally tell clients it's okay if they don't remember their childhood for whatever reason. I tell them, in time, when they're ready, the memories will rise to the surface.

The second reason people get stuck here is because they're on some type of medication, such as antidepressants or anti-anxiety medication, which can cause brain fog and make it hard to remember their childhood. That doesn't mean they can't access these memories, but I have found for some it makes it much harder.

The third reason people get stuck on this step is because they didn't identify Step 2 correctly. This means they didn't connect to the real story they're telling themselves or the underlying theme associated with their current block or challenge.

So, if you're feeling stuck at Step 3 and having trouble finding your earliest memory of the feeling, story, or theme you identified in Step 2, it might be simply because you identified the wrong story. When you are just beginning to use this tool, it can be helpful to have an Inner Mosaic coach support you in the process.

ACTIVITY: DISCOVERING WHEN THIS PART OF YOU WAS BORN

Take some time now to think of your earliest memory about the theme or story you identified in the previous activity. Remember, it might be a completely different situation than your current challenge but the theme is the same.

Write down the details of this earliest memory. What happened? Where were you? What was going on that led to the story or theme you identified in your current situation? Write down as many details as you can remember.

____

____

____

____

____

____

____

____

____

STEP 4: PERSONIFY YOUR PART

The fourth step of the Inner Mosaic method is to personify the part you found in Step 3. This is when you identify your age during your earliest memory. Pick a name for and identify the characteristics, personality, values, beliefs, friends, activities, likes, and dislikes of this part of you.

How old were you at the time of your earliest memory? What would you like to call this younger version of yourself? Did you have a nickname back then? If you could use two or three words to describe your personality back then, what would they be? What were you like—your values, beliefs, likes, and dislikes? Who were your friends, and what were your favorite activities?

In essence, we want to paint a picture of who you were at the time of your earliest memory because this part of you will show up anytime you experience a similar feeling to the original event.

The Bus

The way I like to describe it is to imagine you're driving a bus. It could be a tour bus or a school bus, but it's pretty big. At any given moment, a certain part of you is driving your bus. Sometimes it's the you right now who's had a wealth of experiences. Other times, a younger, less skilled version of you finds a way to jump into the driver's seat.

Have you ever experienced a time when you felt you were not in control of your own thoughts, feelings, and actions? For example, have you ever been so angry or hurt by someone that you attacked them? Maybe not physically, but verbally. You put them down, you hit them where it hurts most (emotionally), and you were on defense or even in revenge mode. Can you relate? Well, if you said no, think of another scenario where you felt you had very little control over yourself. I know we have all experienced some version of this. If you said yes, and since you're reading this book, I think it's safe to say you don't like the feeling of being out of control. Although the part of you that's triggered can get shit done, it's not a fun feeling afterward knowing you just said or did some unkind things.

If you've ever felt like you lost control of your bus, using the Inner Mosaic method is really going to help regain your power.

Take Claire for example. I worked with her for two years, and we discovered her beautiful Inner Mosaic. We formed an Inner Mosaic Map by discovering a new part of her each time she was feeling stuck in her relationship or some other area. I'll share her map with you in a moment, but first let's look at how we used the Inner Mosaic method to support her in transforming her relationships.

When Claire first came to me, she had just embarked on a journey of self-discovery. Her children were almost adults, and she was working up the courage to file for divorce. She had moved to Oahu from the Big Island and brought her two teenage children with her to start fresh.

After divorcing, Claire was hesitant about committing to another relationship, fearing she'd be hurt again. One day, she was reunited with an old male friend, and something clicked. She felt seen for the first time in years. This old friend, whom she knew back in high school, confessed his feelings for Claire from their youth. Soon, Claire found herself in a secret relationship, afraid her family, friends, and children would find out and disapprove.

Claire also didn't want to tell anyone about her relationship because she still didn't know if she wanted to be in one. What we discovered through our work together was she had a very strong Inner Mosaic part who frequently jumped into the driver's seat on her bus and took over. Claire named this part CJ. CJ was a survivor.

In her early twenties, Claire's experiences had hardened her. She really felt lost and alone at the time. She found herself homeless, jumping from couch to couch, and felt abandoned by her family. This version of Claire said "F-you" to the world and her family by being super-independent and tough. Crying wasn't allowed, even after she was raped by someone she thought she could trust. That was the moment CJ was born. I say born because this traumatic moment and series of events left a major imprint on her soul. When an event leaves such an imprint, a new version of yourself is born.

Claire didn't discover this part of herself until her mid-forties. In our sessions together, we realized CJ was the part of Claire who pushed away the people who loved her. CJ was scared of getting hurt again. She had every right to be scared—she had been assaulted and taken advantage of. Of course, she was scared.

And when CJ jumped into the driver's seat, Claire would lose control of her thoughts, feelings, and actions.

So much so, CJ broke up with Claire's boyfriend dozens of times and said really mean things to him.

But what we also found was that CJ was actually protecting not only herself, but an even younger version of Claire, the seven-year-old little girl who was taught by her parents that "The people you love are the people who can hurt you." At age seven, Claire was being bullied and felt abandoned, rejected, and outcast. We called this part of Claire "Sista C." Sista C became a people pleaser and learned shining her light brightly only put more of a target on her back and made others feel uncomfortable.

Claire and I used the Inner Mosaic method to create her Inner Mosaic Map using moments when she felt stuck or when she found herself bumping up against unwanted thoughts, feelings, or actions in relationships. An Inner Mosaic Map is simply a list of all the Inner Mosaic parts that we discovered over time and mapped out to use as a reference for future challenges. Here's Claire's Inner Mosaic Map we created while working together:

1
Big Sis
4 years old
Proactive. In 6th grade I got into a fight with an older boy. Can show up as "Mama Bear" now as an adult.

2
Sista C
7 years old
Outgoing. Was bullied. Felt abandoned, rejected and outcast. People pleaser and didn't want to outshine anyone. My parents told me, "only people you love can hurt you."

3
Heart Breaker
16 years old
"Broke-up" with those who got to close to me.

4
CJ
Early 20's
Raped, didn't cry, tough, and said, "F-you" by being independent and tough.

5
Good Wife
21-44 years old
Met hubby, became Christian, got married at 21, obeyed to be a "good wife." Felt inauthentic for half my life.

6
Bad Mom
44 years old
Left controlling, toxic marriage. Began finding myself. Lots of mom guilt. First time in 22 years I felt like my authentic self.

7
BCC
Now
Blossomed. Found my passion and pursued it. Lots of healing and empowerment.

Now that you've seen Claire's Inner Mosaic Map, you too can create your own map to help you identify who is showing up whenever you're facing a challenge or feeling stuck in your life or relationships. Make sure you complete steps 4 through 6 in the Inner Mosaic method and add those details to your map when you're done.

ACTIVITY: PERSONIFYING YOUR PART

You have identified the current situation you're feeling challenged by, you are aware of the theme or story you have attached to the situation, and you have found your earliest memory that fits the theme of what's happening in your life. Now comes the fun part!

Take a moment to answer the following questions through the lens of your earliest memory to personify the part of yourself that's currently driving the bus:

- How old were you at the time of your earliest memory?
- What would you like to call this younger version of yourself?
- Did you have a nickname back then?
- If you could use two or three words to describe your personality back then, what would they be?

- What were you like—your values, beliefs, likes, and dislikes?
- Who were your friends, and what were your favorite activities?

Remember, the parts of you that show up and want to drive the bus are just as complex and cool as the you of today. People are multidimensional beings with complex personas. And so are all the different parts of you. Use the space below or a journal to write down any other memories you have about yourself at the age you identified.

____

____

____

____

____

____

____

____

____

Breaking the Cycle of Insanity

One of the most common questions I get is, "How do I stop feeling this way?" Most of my clients are actually looking for more control over their emotions. They're sick of their spouse, a family member, or anyone else controlling their feelings. Allowing any situation to dictate how you think, feel, or act is very disempowering.

Understanding your Inner Mosaic can help you interrupt the automatic subconscious patterns that no longer serve you. The last two steps of the Inner Mosaic method empower you to do just that.

STEP 5: ACKNOWLEDGE WHO'S DRIVING YOUR BUS

In the fifth step of the Inner Mosaic method, it's important to acknowledge the part of you that has jumped into the driver's seat. In Steps 1 through 4, you figured out *who* this part of you is. But the most important thing to do now is take the time to acknowledge them rather than yelling and screaming at them to metaphorically get out of the driver's seat.

I am aware a younger version of myself is driving the bus right now, and this younger version is simply scared of getting hurt again.

Do you like being told what to do? Do you like someone yelling and screaming at you, treating you like you don't belong or you're incompetent?

I'm going to guess you replied with a big fat *no*.

Exactly. So instead of yelling, screaming, criticizing, or belittling yourself by telling yourself, "Stop acting like a child" or "You're being crazy," try being kind to yourself.

Think of it this way for a moment. Do you know a child around the same age as the Inner Mosaic part you identified in Steps 1 through 4? It could be your own child, a relative, or even a family friend. No matter who it is, I'm guessing if they found themselves in a situation where they felt stuck, frustrated, hurt, or sad, you'd comfort them and allow them to have their feelings.

Then why is it that when a younger version of ourselves has similar feelings, we criticize, ridicule, or exile this part of ourselves? If you can relate to this, you're not alone. Many, including myself, have been hypercritical of our younger self. I glance back at past experiences and judge myself from my current level of awareness.

"You should've known better."

"How could you be so stupid?"

"What were you thinking?"

No one likes to be yelled at, criticized, or ridiculed. It only causes more frustration, heartache, and suffering. Instead, I invite you to shine a kinder eye on your thoughts, feelings, and actions as if they were that of a child, teen, or even a young adult. No matter their age, remember what that stage of life was like and all the things you didn't know about yet.

When you can do that, the part of you being triggered in your current situation will feel seen. Once they feel seen, it's time to listen.

ACTIVITY: ACKNOWLEDGING THE DRIVER

This step is the simplest but most transformative. Just say to yourself out loud, "I am aware that a younger version of myself is driving the bus right now, and this younger version of me is simply scared of getting hurt again."

STEP 6: SUPPORT THIS PART OF YOURSELF IN THE CURRENT SITUATION

The final step of the Inner Mosaic method is to ask your younger self what they need from you (the wiser, more evolved self) in your *current* situation. Some examples of the things your Inner Mosaic part might need could be words of wisdom, comfort, validation, or even giving yourself a hug that can look like squeezing a pillow or even asking for a hug from a loved one.

What do you need at this moment? How can I support you?

Early on, this step can take some time. It's best done with an Inner Mosaic coach or a skilled professional. The goal of this step is to build trust between the different parts of yourself. And in fact, the ultimate goal of the entire Inner Mosaic method is to build trust between all the parts of yourself. Once you trust all the parts of yourself and all the parts of yourself trust you, life begins to happen *through* you and *as* you.

But let me make a little distinction between inner child work and the Inner Mosaic method. When I was in school, my understanding of inner child work was to go back to the experience your younger self had and heal that situation by comforting and consoling yourself and creating a new storyline in that original moment. In the Inner Mosaic method, it's important to understand we aren't going back and changing the story of the past. We aren't healing our inner child. We are honoring and acknowledging that younger version of ourselves and trusting the wisdom we've gained from their experience. And from that perspective, we're recognizing they're still here with us in the present moment trying to keep us safe and stop us from repeating any mistakes we made in the past.

If you haven't noticed by now, we aren't really fixing, solving, or resolving any of our problems from the past. We are staying in the present because the only time that truly exists is *now*. And we are also not focused on fixing, solving, or resolving any problems outside of ourselves. The reality is all our problems exist *within*! If we can resolve the *inner* conflict, and learn how to generate our own feelings despite the circumstances, we can overcome any challenge we face.

ACTIVITY: OFFERING YOUR SUPPORT

Take some time to identify what your Inner Mosaic part needs right now in this current situation. If you're not sure, try some things out to see if they help. Just remember this step may feel funny at first—and that's okay.

The Inner Mosaic method takes time to learn and apply. Keep coming back to this chapter every time you're feeling stuck or frustrated. As I mentioned earlier, this can become one of your greatest awareness and alignment tools.

This process continues to help my clients in their relationships both with themselves and others. Once you begin to master this method, you unlock an unmatched feeling of empowerment. Then, you will begin to have more dominion over your life (and your outcomes).

Chapter 9

The Art of Forgiveness

*"To forgive is to set a prisoner free and discover that
the prisoner was you."*

— *Lewis B. Smedes*

One of the most rigorous tasks you will ever undertake is the practice of forgiveness. What many don't quite understand is that forgiveness is the act of exchanging one thought, feeling, story, or meaning for another. If you haven't noticed already, much of the Inner Mosaic method really is a forgiveness practice and process.

Earlier, I introduced four new beliefs I invited you to take on to transform any relationship. By simply giving up a former belief for the new ones I introduced, you were practicing forgiveness. For-give is the act of *giving up* one thing *for* another; giving up one belief for another *is* a form of forgiveness.

In the Triple A's of Transformation, I shared a simple yet powerful process of Awareness, Alignment, and Action. This, too, is a forgiveness process. When you become aware of something new, be it a thought, feeling, action, or outcome, you have the opportunity to transform yourself

114

and the world around you. With your new awareness, you connect with your highest and best self and take action to serve your new awareness. This also is giving up one thought, feeling, or action for another more aligned one.

Finally, I taught you how to identify your Inner Mosaic parts, create an Inner Mosaic Map and use it to help overcome any challenge you might bump up against. This, too, in fact, is a forgiveness process. You see, when you shine a kind eye on your younger self, learn to listen deeply, love unconditionally, and wholeheartedly trust all the different parts of yourself, you are giving up an old and outdated view of yourself for a new, more empowered one.

I love what Marianne Williamson wrote in her book *A Return To Love*, "Every act is either a call for love or an expression of love no matter how unskilled it may appear." This single quote has helped me transcend many relationships. Learning to understand everyone is doing the best they can with what they have at any given moment really takes the hurt and pain out of what I felt people were doing *to* me. I realized deep down inside each person is a pure soul made of pure love. And my willingness to see this part of each person who had "wronged" me was not a gift for them, but a gift to myself.

As one of my mentors, Mary Morrissey, says, "All forgiveness is self-forgiveness." And I believe this is true with all my being. Remember when I said earlier all your challenges and "problems" are within yourself? The key to solving these problems is forgiveness. Once you can forgive yourself, it's much easier to forgive others. The same goes for love. Once you learn to love yourself, it's much easier to love and be loved.

I can preach forgiveness all day, but it does nothing for us until we put it into practice. Here's an exercise that really helped me in the forgiveness process.

THE LOVE LETTER

When I was in the thick of my marital challenges, I decided to write a love letter to my husband Denver as a forgiveness practice. It wasn't just any love letter—this love letter was specific and not necessarily meant for his eyes.

I learned about this forgiveness practice while I was working in the substance use treatment field. One of the assignments we gave our clients was something called "A Love Letter." We had them write this letter to someone they held resentment toward, and we had them read it in their individual counseling sessions.

I later learned this exercise was created by John Gray, PhD, and he wrote about it in his book *Men Are from Mars, Women Are from Venus.* It's actually called "The Feeling

Letter Technique." Most of the following instructions come from his original work with some adaptations taken from the treatment facility where I learned this technique and some adaptations of my own.

This is a transformative process I encourage you to take the time to complete. Pause for a moment to grab your journal and think about whom you need to forgive. When you're ready, here is the outline and instructions for this technique.

Love Letter Guidelines

1. Begin by expressing your anger, resentment, and blame. Allow yourself to move through the other feelings until you get down to love.
2. Each love letter has five parts. Use the lead in phrases (see below) to help if you get stuck on one part and need to move to the next.
3. Write your letter using "I" statements to keep the focus on how *you* are feeling or what *you* are experiencing.
4. End each section with "I want…."
5. Keep the sections balanced. Write a few sentences for each section of the letter. Don't spend too much time on any one section.

6. Don't try to be rational. Feelings are irrational, and you don't have to justify them. Just let your hand do the writing, put your brain on hold, and write from your heart.

7. Do not stop writing your letter until you get through all the sections. Always complete "A Love Letter" in one sitting. Set a time limit. Thirty minutes should suffice.

8. Sign your name at the end.

Important Tips: (read before writing your letter)

1. The primary purpose is for the writer to feel better, not to change someone.

2. Start writing the letter at whichever level of feeling you are experiencing. Then, at some point, move up to anger, then back through the other feelings.

3. "A Love Letter" is a successful tool for healing past upsets.

4. You can teach children to write love letters. You can make "easy-to-write" forms and have the kids fill in the blanks.

5. Try writing a love letter to yourself, but *do not* use it as an excuse to beat yourself up.

6. Try writing a love letter for another person, taking their point of view in a conflict you are having with them. Then share the letter with them.

7. You and your partner (or loved one) can write each other a love letter. Go into a separate quiet place so you won't be affected by the other's presence. If you choose to share your letters with one another, it's recommended to do it with the support of a trained professional.

8. "Monster" love letters are very lengthy and have excessive anger. *Do not* share these with the person you are writing to—they will most likely be hurt and push you away. You can share this with a supportive friend, coach, or therapist to help you process your feelings even further.

9. Don't use a love letter to "dump" on someone.

10. You may want to save your letters for future reference.

11. Prior to sharing your love letter with anyone, take into consideration how the other person might respond to your letter. Will they be able to listen past the anger? What is the reason you want to share your letter with them? Is it to express all of your feelings? Is the goal to feel heard? Are you wanting a deeper connection with this person? Take time to think about these questions before you decide to share your letter with the other person.

12. *Pro Tip: Write your love letter with the intention of burning it or throwing it away after you write it, and see if that changes how you write your letter.*

How to Write a Love Letter

Dear ______________,

I am writing this letter to share my feelings with you.

1. **ANGER** (and blame)

    I don't like it when…

    I feel frustrated when…

    I feel annoyed when…

    I am angry because…

    I resent…

    I hate it when…

    I'm fed up with…

    I'm tired of…

    I *want*…

2. **SADNESS** (and hurt)

    I feel disappointed because…

    I am sad because…

    I feel awful because…

    I feel hurt because…

    I wanted…

    I *want*…

3. FEAR (and insecurity)

> I feel worried…
>
> I am afraid…
>
> I feel scared…
>
> I don't want…
>
> I don't understand…
>
> I need…
>
> I *want*…

4. RESPONSIBILITY (guilt and remorse)

> I feel embarrassed…
>
> I am sorry I…
>
> I am sorry for…
>
> I feel ashamed…
>
> I didn't mean to…
>
> I didn't want…
>
> Please forgive me for…
>
> I *want*…

5. LOVE (forgiveness, understanding, and desire)

> I love you because…
>
> I love when…
>
> I love…
>
> I appreciate…
>
> I thank you for…

I understand…
I forgive you for…
I know…
I am willing to…
I *want*…

Sign your name.

You can use so many other exercises, rituals, and practices to bring more forgiveness into your life. The main point here is to just start somewhere.

As the old saying goes, when you hold onto resentments, it's like drinking poison and hoping the other person will die. I know sometimes forgiving is the hardest thing you will ever do. But I want you to know when you forgive someone, you're not letting them off the hook or saying what they did was okay. Forgiving someone is also not saying you will forget what happened.

A Course in Miracles says, "Forgiveness removes a block in me to my awareness of love's presence." That's key to healing, to happiness, and to a life well lived. Letting love into your life. Letting your life be filled with love. Coming from love. None of these are possible if you continue to hold onto resentments in your relationships.

Let it go or let it be. Either way, it's no longer your burden to carry. Let the hurt, pain, anger, and frustration go. Release it to something greater than yourself. Remember earlier we talked about your Spiritual Truths—whoever or whatever you believe in is out there supporting you. Give it to them. Give it to God.

Letting go is the only way to be ready to receive the good that's meant to come to you next.

FORGIVENESS AND YOUR INNER MOSAIC

As repeated over and over in this book, the ultimate goal in the Inner Mosaic method is to love and trust all parts of yourself. To do that, you will need to forgive the parts of yourself you still don't trust.

Going back to the bus analogy, at any given moment, a part of us is driving our own bus. Sometimes, the part that gets triggered by the current situation might be a very young version of ourselves. That can cause many to panic.

It's one thing to become aware a seven-year-old is driving the bus, but being okay with them driving is a whole different story—to trust they know what they're doing and are capable of driving the bus, even if it's just for a moment.

The other form of forgiveness needed is between your younger self and your present self. That the younger version of yourself jumped into the driver's seat in the first place means they don't trust *you* to drive either. It's very important that all the versions of yourself trust the you of *today*. The only way to do that is to tap into your younger self and begin the forgiveness process from that perspective. Who is it you, as a child, need to forgive? What anger, resentment, fear, or frustration is holding your younger self back from truly letting go and trusting everything is working out for your highest and best good?

Take some time to journal and explore this question. It won't be easy and the answers won't always come quickly. As I mentioned earlier, forgiveness is a practice, not a destination. It's not a one-and-done thing. If you're still alive and breathing, you will always have something to forgive in others or yourself.

A great way to maintain a healthy heart and mind is to think of forgiveness as a daily hygiene practice. A healthy forgiveness practice is the same as brushing your teeth each day. Take time to reflect and forgive yourself and others at the end of every day. Whether you're reflecting on something you can do better tomorrow or someone you could shine a kinder glance upon, taking time to reflect will help you maintain a healthy forgiveness practice.

Chapter 10
Metaphysics and Mental Science

"If you want to find the secrets of the universe, think in terms of energy, frequency, and vibration."

— Nikola Tesla

As we draw our exploration of Alignment to a close, it's important to recognize the subtle yet powerful undercurrents shaping our understanding of ourselves and the world around us. The fabric of our existence is intricately woven with threads of both the tangible and the intangible—inviting us into the realm of the metaphysical. We'll first touch on Universal Laws and Spiritual Truths, the fundamental principles that, knowingly or unknowingly, influence our lives. Next, we'll talk about our mental faculties, the very core of how we perceive and respond to the world. And, to wrap it up, we'll explore the transformative power of meditation and mantras.

This chapter serves as a bridge, connecting the practical with the profound. While these concepts might sound a bit abstract at first, their real-world applications and influence are undeniable. By understanding these elements, we gain dominion over our lives and relationships. So, let's dive in and uncover the wisdom that awaits.

EMBARKING ON A SPIRITUAL JOURNEY

In the heart-wrenching aftermath of that life-changing morning when I realized Denver had been lying to me for years, I felt an overpowering need to find meaning and to get answers. I needed to know if my marriage was going to last. Not knowing was torturous. So many of my clients have experienced this unbearable pain too. And they also sought answers. Out of desperation, even though it terrified me, I went to see a psychic.

I don't know that I fully believed in psychics at that time, but I knew they would give me some sort of answer. And because the lens of religion left me struggling to believe in the unseen world, I went looking for answers in the metaphysical world.

Although I was hesitant to share this metaphysical part of my story in this book, I decided it was an important part of my journey, and after working with many other women, I realized it was part of their story as well. This metaphysical part of our journey we tend to keep private and don't really want others to know about. Maybe it's because psychics and metaphysics in general contradict religious beliefs or maybe it's the fear of being shamed or seen differently by those around us, *or* maybe, like the me of the past, we are secretly fascinated by the metaphysical world, but we are paralyzed by fear of the unknown.

Let's get to it, shall we?

I spoke to two different psychics. Neither gave me good news about my marriage and what was coming. My first encounter with a psychic was right after I found out about Denver's addiction. A friend wanted to talk to a psychic for fun, so we scheduled sessions to see what he had to say about our lives. At the time, I didn't take the reading too seriously, but I wrote down his prediction of what each of the next twelve months of my life would look like in my notebook.

A year went by without looking at those notes. But after our failed marriage therapy experience, my desire to know increased tenfold. I wanted to know if all this work I was putting into myself and my marriage was going to pay off, I wanted to know if my husband was ever going to change, and I wanted to know if I would ever be happy—I wanted to feel a sense of certainty again.

I decided I was going to get another reading. But before I called to make an appointment, I went back to my notebook to read my notes from the last reading, which was almost exactly one year earlier. As I read the month-by-month predictions about what would happen, I was shocked. It was spot on! My life had unfolded exactly as he had predicted. Remember, I didn't look at these notes all year, and actually forgot most of what he had said.

When I talked to him the second time, his words held more weight. I knew he was gifted and that everything he told me would likely come true too.

He validated my fears, and my heart was broken. In short, the psychic told me my career would be fine; I was doing well at work. But my husband would never change, and we would likely be divorced by the end of the year. But the worst thing the psychic told me was my youngest daughter would likely become an addict like my husband when she grew up.

Talk about stabbing a mother in the heart. I was shocked. There was nothing I could say or think of saying at that point. I was no longer focused on getting divorced by the end of the year. I was worried about my daughter.

When I shared my reading with close friends, they told me about another psychic reader who was well known in my community. I decided to book another reading—I guess you could say to get a second opinion.

The second psychic told me all my daughters are highly gifted and my youngest is the most sensitive to energy.

He confirmed much of what I knew in my heart. When my youngest daughter entered any room, even as young as a few months old, she could put a smile on everyone's face. At the same time, she could also tell if something was off in someone or someplace. She would instantly begin screaming uncontrollably until we moved away from the person or got out of the space.

As a substance use counselor at the time, I believed all my clients were highly sensitive souls. They were simply misguided and not encouraged to embrace their gifts, so they self-medicated and used substances to suppress their sensitivities.

And then it clicked. That's exactly what the first psychic meant when he said my daughter would become an addict. He simply meant if my daughter didn't learn to embrace her gifts, she would be like many of my clients and end up trying to suppress her sensitivities with drugs, alcohol, or other vices.

At that moment, I decided I not only wanted to embark on a spiritual journey to find *my* Spiritual Truths, but I wanted to better understand my gifts and sensitivities so I could help my daughters understand theirs.

I was also determined to prove the first psychic wrong. I wouldn't be divorced by the end of the year, and my daughter would *not* become an addict. And if for whatever reason she did, I would know I had done everything I could to support her in embracing the amazing being she is.

What happened next was a whirlwind adventure into the unknown. I followed every breadcrumb as if I were on a magical, mystical treasure hunt. I began by studying the works of Louise Hay, a cancer survivor and one of the first female leaders in the self-healing movement. Her work on healing the body through affirmations and mantras intrigued me, especially after I had gone through the traumatic experience of my heart condition. Her teachings helped me make sense of what I had gone through and *why* I had gone through it.

After immersing myself in Louise Hay's teachings, I embarked on a spiritual internship. And despite getting in touch with some of my healing abilities from past lives, I still sensed a gap in my understanding. Further exploration introduced me to oracle cards, crystals, sound healing, and more.

Divination, a once foreign term, became a method to connect with the Universal Oneness. Oracle and tarot cards became beacons in my darker moments, with each card's message resonating profoundly. Crystals, nature's wonders, became my healing companions. Their beauty and innate power fascinated me. I pursued a crystal healing certification, appreciating their natural allure as much as their healing attributes.

Okay, let's take some time to unpack what I just wrote in a more universal way.

UNIVERSAL LAWS AND SPIRITUAL TRUTHS

Although I believe both Spiritual Truths and Universal Laws are the same thing, I think it's important to pull them apart for just a moment.

We already addressed two Universal Laws earlier: the Law of Thinking and the Law of Systems.

In the Law of Thinking, you learned your thoughts become things, and ultimately, your results are a perfect reflection of your beliefs. In the Law of Systems, you learned if you change one part of a system, the rest of the system must accommodate and adapt to the initial change to maintain homeostasis or the entire system will come to a natural completion.

When you're in the alignment phase of the Triple A's of Transformation, it's helpful to remember these two laws. They will bring you back to the awareness that life is happening *through* you so you can connect with the infinite side of your nature.

ACTIVITY: IDENTIFYING YOUR SPIRITUAL TRUTHS

I have shared the spiritual journey I embarked on. Now it's time for you to take your own spiritual inventory to see which Spiritual Truths resonate with you. Although both Universal Laws and Spiritual Truths operate whether you believe in them or not, it's still important to remember you are and always will be the highest authority in your own life. You, like all of us, have free will, and it's up to you and the rest of us to accept or reject any belief.

Take a moment here to pause, look to your inner wisdom, and reflect on your beliefs. Here are a few questions to help in the journaling process:

- Did you grow up in a particular religion?
- What did your parents teach you about spirituality or religion?
- What did you like?
- What didn't you like?
- What are your current spiritual beliefs and practices?
- What are your spiritual curiosities and questions? In other words, do you have any unanswered questions or things you're still unsure about?

I want you to take time to journal about these questions because 99 percent of my clients have some sort of disconnect from their spirituality when they first come to me. And if you're reading this book, it's likely you, too, have at least a couple of unanswered spiritual questions.

Now that you've taken time to journal and connect to your current spiritual understanding, it's likely your curiosity is ignited. I want to present two spiritual beliefs to see if they resonate with you. If so, you can use these Spiritual Truths to remain *aligned* with your Highest Self. If not, you can leave them right here on the page where you found them.

The first comes from a quote by French Jesuit priest, scientist, paleontologist, theologian, philosopher, and teacher Pierre Teilhard de Chardin: "We are spiritual beings having a human experience." Let's take a moment to pull this apart for those who may question this beautiful truth.

We have a body, but we are *not* our bodies. For instance, when someone loses a limb, they're still a whole person. A part of their body may be missing, but it doesn't make them any less of a person.

This situation shows us we have an energy, a spirit, and an essence that cannot be lost when a part of our body no longer exists or works. It works the opposite way as well. When someone has dementia, their body may still be intact and functioning, but their mind or spirit may be slipping away. Again, this situation implies we have a body, but we are not our body.

We are an energetic, spiritual, vibrational frequency navigating this human life using what I like to call an earth suit or a physical body. So much science validating

Spiritual Truth exists that I no longer need to talk about it in theory. However, I will allow you to do your own research if you need to accept this belief.

The second Spiritual Truth I want to discuss is the concept of soul families and soulmates. This topic can be a little more controversial and subjective since the scientific research backing this truth is still minimal. However, I have always taught my clients they're the highest authority in their lives and so are you. So, as I mentioned before, take what you like and leave the rest.

Soul families are simply souls you incarnate with over and over again. In essence, following the belief we are all one and we all come from the same source, everyone is from the same soul family. However, in this context, I am simply identifying a group of souls who tend to incarnate on earth together.

Let me take a step back for a moment. Some people don't believe in past lives for various reasons, including religious beliefs. Some people are open, but they don't know enough about it to have a stance. Here's what I believe—see if it resonates with you: I believe our souls incarnate on earth many times. I believe the earth is simply a playground or experience center for souls. As spiritual beings, we can't experience physical touch or the polarities of life. In the human experience, we can have these experiences and feel sad, mad, or anxious, as well as happy, joyous, or thrilled, all in a single day or even within moments.

Many books have been written on this topic if you want to explore more. Here, though, I simply want to introduce you to the topic of soul families and soulmates.

If you believe each soul can have many human (or non-human) lives, you might also believe in soul families. Have you ever felt you have known someone forever, even if it was the very first time you met them? That person could be someone in your soul family.

I also want to discuss soulmates. My personal definition and understanding of soulmates is two souls who are strongly tethered over multiple lifetimes. Sometimes your soulmate can be your best friend, while other times they're your spouse or even family, like a parent or child. I believe your soulmate can manifest differently in every lifetime, and they often have a soul contract with you.

What is a soul contract?

A soul contract is a pre-incarnation agreement between two souls. Either one or both want a specific experience in a given lifetime and the other soul agrees to play a specific role to help facilitate the experience.

For example, Denver and I are certainly soulmates. No matter how many times we are pulled apart, we somehow find a way back to each other. I believe in my heart we have incarnated together many times, and sometimes we are partners while in other lifetimes we play different roles for each other. I also believe Denver signed a soul contract with me to be unwavering in his ways so I can learn a lesson and have a specific experience I wanted in this lifetime. For me, I think our contract states that Denver is *not* to change just because I asked him to. He is also my grounding source and keeps me from floating off into the clouds.

You see, Denver is here to help me learn to be the best version of myself and prepare me for the later lessons and opportunities in my lifetime.

Overall, these Spiritual Truths have helped me *realign* with my highest self. In those dark hours of my life, knowing I have a soul family and a soulmate who are here to help me experience life's greatest gifts has been my saving grace. I know it can be yours too.

THE CONCEPT OF MENTAL FACULTIES

The concept of mental faculties here differs somewhat from the standard idea of cerebral function many think of when discussing mental capacities.

I was introduced to the concept of mental faculties a few years ago by my mentors Mary Morrissey and the late Bob Proctor. They learned about them from Dr. Thurman

Fleet. Learning about these mental faculties helped me further transform my marriage.

I didn't discover my mental faculties during the dark night of my soul. Although I had some innate knowledge of these faculties through my studies in psychology, I didn't know I was actually using them.

The six mental faculties are Intuition, Imagination, Memory, Will, Perception, and Reason. Although each is equally important and can help us align ourselves to our Spiritual Truths, I will emphasize the faculties that made the biggest difference in my life and my relationships.

Intuition

Activist and spiritual teacher Ma Jaya once said, "Quiet the mind and the soul will speak." Your soul speaking sounds lovely, right? This is what many people refer to as intuition. Intuition is one of the mental faculties we have access to in this human experience. It's a wonderful alignment tool to help tune in to your highest truth. Some people call intuition your "still small voice" or "gut feeling." Ultimately, it's your internal compass and inner knower. Have you ever heard the expression "Your knower knows"? Well, it refers to your intuition.

When I was on my spiritual journey, I learned many different ways to access intuition.

Here are six different ways you might receive your intuitive messages from Source:

1. See—shapes, symbols, orbs, etc.
2. Hear—a voice or sound no one else hears.
3. Taste—a distinct taste.
4. Smell—a scent undetectable by others.
5. Feel—chills are the most common but some have more direct feelings and can even feel sharp or dull pains in certain areas of their body.
6. Know—an instant understanding/knowledge of something without evidence.

Overall, no matter how intuition manifests, I find developing a relationship with intuition helps in every aspect of life. Your intuition is like your internal compass or GPS. Without intuition, all you have is a roadmap drawn by you, your family, and everyone else around you—and it's not always accurate or reliable.

I want to discuss one more thing about intuition before we move on to our next mental faculty—how to discern intuition from empathy.

Few teachers I know of teach this distinction or teach it well, so here's my attempt to help you identify the difference.

First, I believe we live in a loving universe. Everything comes from love and is love—not just the emotional feeling of love, but the deepest meaning of love. That said, I believe love is the only "real" thing.

As *A Course in Miracles* explains, "Only love is real and all else is an illusion."

I believe intuition speaks in the language of love. All other feelings are simply an illusion or what I define as your empathic abilities. I also like to describe intuition as messages from God or the Universe. And if God doesn't "fear" anything, why would God's messages be based in fear? They wouldn't.

So, whenever you get a fear-based message, it's actually coming from the human side of your nature—your empathic abilities. Whether you are sensing your own fears or the fears of others, I want you to know it's *not* intuition.

This is so important because many people I know use intuition as a scapegoat to say, "Oh, I have a bad feeling about this." Well, if it was truly intuition, they would simply receive a message saying "No," "Not now," or even "There's another way." Fear-based messages such as "This isn't a good idea" or "Remember what happened last time?" come from the human side of your nature—your past experiences.

In the context of relationships, I've had clients mistake their fears or empathic responses for intuition. Such a fear sounds like, "I know they're lying to me. I can just feel it."

I did this too. When I found out about Denver's addiction and the lies he told me over the years to keep his double life hidden, I became hypersensitive to subtle clues he might be lying. I thought I was using my intuitive "Spidey sense," but instead, I was simply reading his nervous energy.

As I shared with you earlier, one of the tensest moments of our day was when Denver came home from work. He would walk on eggshells, worried about my mood when he walked through the door. Some days, I tried hard to be nice; other days, I was so frustrated with the kids, I was ready to lash out at him the moment he stepped into the house.

Once I noticed he was walking on eggshells, my "Spidey sense" kicked in—I could tell something was wrong. I would ask if he had smoked before he came home. I would ask about his day. Basically, it was a full-blown interrogation.

That line of questioning, in and of itself, would cause anyone to get nervous and annoyed. So, I picked and poked until Denver got defensive, and then I would say, "Hah! See, I knew you were lying to me. Why are you getting so defensive if you didn't do anything?"

And then we were off to the races.

Here's the thing. My husband wasn't trying to lie to me about anything. That he was nervous about our relationship was enough to validate the "funny feeling" I got every time he walked in the door.

Only after months and months of torturing ourselves did I realize the difference between intuition and empathy. Every time he stepped into the house, I immediately felt his feelings. That's how sensitive I am to other people. I can feel their energy and their feelings. And I'm guessing, if you're reading this book, you are also highly sensitive to others.

That's exactly why it's so important to be able to discern between intuition and empathy. And remember, if all the "evidence" adds up, you're likely feeling others' energy and using past experiences as clues.

On the other hand, normally your intuitive nudges won't make any sense. Learn to listen to find the difference for yourself.

ACTIVITY: ACCESSING YOUR INTUITION

Take a moment to journal some of the ways your intuition speaks to you. Do you get chills when you hear something you know in your heart is true? Is there something you always know before anyone else? For example, a friend of mine knows the gender of someone's baby well before they're able to find out at the doctors. Write down anything that comes to mind that can possibly be your intuition speaking to you. The more you stay open to receiving your intuitive messages, the clearer your messages will come through.

___

Imagination

While intuition allowed me to tap into an unseen guidance system, my imagination provided a canvas upon which I could project my desires and aspirations.

This mental faculty is one of creativity and child-like playfulness. I have found that many, dare I say most, adults have let their mental muscles atrophy. Well, let's say in the purest form of imagination that is. On the other hand, most of my clients, when I first begin working with them, have grown to only use their imagination to terrorize themselves—imagining the worst-case scenario in any given situation.

It's important that we strengthen our imagination muscle in ways that support our growth and expansion rather than living in fear or continuing to play it safe. In Chapter 14, I'll share with you an activity to help improve your mental faculty of imagination, but for now, let's simply reflect on how you have been using your imagination in your life.

ACTIVITY: TAPPING INTO YOUR IMAGINATION

Take some time to journal how you've been using your mental faculty of imagination in your life. Are you anything like me and while driving, you imagine disastrous accidents happening on the road in front of you and all the ways you will avoid the danger and save your family if it were to actually happen? Or do you imagine other worst-case scenarios like my clients? Or are you someone who already uses their imagination to dream up their future and think of all the amazing possibilities that life has to offer? Go ahead, write down a few thoughts about your imagination.

____

____

____

____

____

____

____

____

____

____

____

____

____

Will

While the brilliance of imagination gives us the ability to carve out the compelling blueprint of our desires, bringing our vision to life requires another potent mental faculty: will. If imagination were the artist sketching a masterpiece, then will would be the hand that holds the brush, steadfast and determined.

Diving deep into this journey, I initially mistook will for willpower. But as my understanding evolved, I came to recognize the stark difference between the two. While willpower is a push energy, often stemming from our finite, human resources—like trying to hold a ball underwater for an extended period of time—will is more profound. It's not a force but a gentle command. It arises from the infinite side of our nature, tapping into a reservoir of boundless energy and potential.

This realization was a challenging paradigm shift for me. For years, I'd been leveraging willpower, muscling through situations by sheer determination. But in doing so, I was merely tapping into a finite resource, which left me drained and often defeated when faced with more significant challenges. Mastering the faculty of will was about learning to align with this infinite part of me and command my reality without the forceful push of willpower.

For a whole year, I dedicated myself to this transformation, integrating the Universal Law of Thinking with the mental faculty of will. It became a valuable tool, ensuring that regardless of external circumstances, my internal landscape remained anchored to my vision. I stopped letting the external world dominate my inner sanctum. Instead, my chosen reality, anchored in imagination and held steadfastly by will, began to change my life.

Transitioning from using willpower to harnessing will is transformative. By understanding the gentle, boundless nature of will, you will not only be able to align your actions with your vision but also discover a wellspring of energy and alignment, making your journey toward my goals more harmonious and aligned.

ACTIVITY: HARNESSING THE POWER OF WILL

In essence, will is your ability to hold something at the forefront of your mind without strain or struggle. One way I learned to build my mental muscle of will was through meditation. Take some time to meditate—you can either pause your reading now or set aside some time this week (or daily if you're up for the challenge) to add some guided meditation or simply focus on your breathing.

Here's a simple way to begin your meditation journey:

1. Find a quiet and comfortable space where you won't be interrupted or distracted by anyone or anything.
2. Make sure to use the restroom and drink some water before you begin.
3. Set a timer for 3-5 minutes.
4. Either sit or lie down in a comfortable position. Note that if you lie down, you may fall asleep.
5. Simply focus your attention on your breath. Breathe in slowly through your nose and out through your mouth like you're blowing through a straw.
6. Repeat this for 3-5 minutes.
7. Notice when your thoughts drift away from your breath and gently guide your attention back to your breathing.

Remember that there are many different ways to strengthen your will muscle; this is just one way I have learned to improve my ability to command my mind and stay focused on what's most important to me.

Memory

Having now learned to harness the gentle command of will, ensuring our actions are aligned with our vision, here's our next pivotal mental faculty: memory. At first glance, memory might seem straightforward. It helps us recall the past, after all. Yet this faculty has more depth than just reminiscing. In fact, memory plays a dual role, with both backward and forward functions.

Backward memory connects us to the past. It's the reservoir of experiences, lessons learned, and moments lived. By tapping into it, we can extract wisdom from past trials and triumphs, ensuring their lessons aren't lost, and instead building a foundation for our future growth. This is the mental faculty we are exercising when we recall our earliest memory in the Inner Mosaic method.

Then there's forward memory. It might sound paradoxical—how can one remember something that hasn't happened yet? But this is where memory's synergy with imagination comes into play. While imagination lets us craft a compelling vision of our desired future, forward memory assists in holding on to that vision, embedding it deeply within our psyche. It's like a mental bookmark ensuring we always have quick access to the future we've envisioned.

The harmony between these two types of memory is crucial. While it's beneficial to reflect on our past experiences, it's equally vital not to become tethered to them, especially if they don't serve our present or future aspirations. That's where our mental faculty of will comes into play. It reminds us to stay rooted in our envisioned future rather than getting entangled in bygones. This alignment between will, forward memory, and imagination creates a powerful trifecta, propelling us toward our goals while ensuring we remain grounded in the lessons of the past.

Reason

From the dual nature of memory, we move on to another multifaceted mental faculty: reason. At its core, reason is our capacity to think, understand, and form judgments logically. But much like the two facets of memory, reason also exists in two states: ordinary and extraordinary.

Ordinary reason relies heavily on our five senses. It's the pragmatic side of our cognitive process, where we use tangible evidence from our surroundings or situation to make sense of events. It's the analytical part of us that needs to see to believe, to touch to verify, and to hear to confirm.

Extraordinary reason, on the other hand, ventures beyond the confines of the sensory and the tangible. It's a deeper, more intuitive form of understanding, pulling insights not from the world around us but from a vast, unseen realm. Here, we aren't limited by the physical and the immediately observable. We lean on something greater, an expansive universe of possibility that ordinary reason might dismiss as implausible. Intuition often employs this extraordinary reasoning. Have you ever felt a deep-seated instinct (gut feeling) you couldn't logically explain, yet you felt compelled to trust it? That's intuition working in tandem with extraordinary reason.

Tapping into extraordinary reason requires faith—a faith not tethered to any one religion but a broader, non-denominational belief in the unseen. This kind of faith isn't about adhering to specific dogmas but embracing trust in a force greater than oneself. Whether we call it the Universe, God, Nature, or any other name, it's the conscious decision to believe there's an order, a guiding force, and a bigger picture than our five senses alone can grasp. It challenges us to move beyond the need for immediate evidence and trust in the vastness of what we might not see but can undoubtedly feel.

In the quest to save my marriage, extraordinary reason often took the lead, urging me to lean on spiritual insights and intuitive nudges even when the tangible world seemed to suggest doing otherwise. It was a profound lesson in faith, trust, and the boundless possibilities of the Universe.

Perception

Having navigated the realms of both ordinary and extraordinary reason, we now turn our attention to another important mental faculty: perception. In fact, we spent a whole chapter on the power of perception. But let's take another moment to appreciate this mental faculty and unpack it.

If reason is our ability to process and understand, perception is the lens through which we view, interpret, and ultimately give meaning to the world around us. Our perceptions are deeply powerful. They shape our reactions, our emotions, and the narratives we construct about our experiences. While reason works to understand, perception allows us to see things from different angles, offering diverse viewpoints on a single situation. It grants us the freedom to choose how we want to interpret an event, the meaning we assign to it, and consequently, how we feel about it.

Consider the analogy of the beach ball. When a multicolored, striped beach ball is positioned between two people so each is looking at a different side, this simple object can be the source of two entirely different perceptions. One might see stripes of blue and white, while the other sees red and yellow. Neither is incorrect; they're just viewing the ball from different perspectives—

one from the right side of the ball and the other from the left. Similarly, situations present themselves where two individuals might experience the same event but walk away with contrasting interpretations. It's not about who's right or wrong but about acknowledging the multifaceted nature of experiences.

In my journey, especially in the mission to transform my marriage, understanding the power of perception was invaluable. It taught me that challenges, setbacks, or disagreements weren't necessarily negative. Instead, they were opportunities to shift my lens, to try to see things from a different perspective, perhaps even through my partner's eyes. By adjusting my perception, I could reframe challenges into opportunities and misunderstandings into learning experiences. This ability to shift perspective, to choose a more empowering or empathetic viewpoint, became a tool for transformation, allowing me to approach hurdles with a more constructive and understanding mindset.

In reflecting on the tapestry of our minds, it's evident these mental faculties are the threads that weave together our inner worlds. From intuition guiding us, imagination inspiring us, will maintaining our focus, memory keeping us anchored, reason enlightening us, to perception offering us varied views, each mental faculty has a unique role, yet they operate in unison. As I strove to save my marriage, leaning into each of these faculties provided clarity, direction, and resilience. I hope sharing their significance with you helps you harness their collective power, understanding a potent arsenal lies within you, ready to navigate life's complexities and embrace its wonders.

MEDITATION AND MANTRAS

Another tool I often used on my spiritual journey to help me stay aligned with my highest self was meditation and mantras. I used to think they were these torturous things people did to themselves. I could not wrap my brain around sitting still in silence for hours on end. It looked like a waste of time.

However, in my darkest moments, I turned to meditation to guide me out of the suffering I was living in and into the land of light, love, and solutions.

I began my journey with guided meditations. I learned my soul wanders quickly, so I needed twice as many grounding cords as others. But nonetheless, these guided meditations helped me to focus within.

Mantras were also a very powerful part of my spiritual practice and still are. Slightly different from affirmations, mantras are more universal statements that help you reconnect to the infinite power all around you.

Here are some of my favorites:

- "I am the keeper of my mind and body. Wherever love is present, fear is a stranger. And love is here (or I am love)." — Kyle Gray
- This is what it looks like while it's all working out.
- This is life happening *through* me.
- This or something better still.
- "There is only one thing happening at any given moment and that's Infinite Intelligence." — Kirsten Welles
- "Every act is either a call *for* love or an expression *of* love, no matter how unskilled it may appear." — Marianne Williamson
- I walk in faith, and live in love.
- "God grant me the serenity to accept the things I cannot change, the courage to change the things I can, and the wisdom to know the difference." — Serenity Prayer
- I am a spiritual being having a human experience.
- The divine in me honors and sees the divine in you.
- What gift am I being presented with today?
- How can I grow from this?
- My partner is a perfect reflection of my beliefs—so what belief or story am I subscribing to? And what story would I love instead?
- It only takes one person to transform a relationship, and I am the change agent.

- That was then, this is now.
- Today is a brand-new baby day!
- What would love do here?
- Is this coming from a place of love or fear?
- Up until now… [insert an unwanted experience]. (Add this phrase in front of any sentence that you are experiencing but no longer want to have moving forward. For example, up until now…my relationship has been my biggest challenge or stress in my life.)
- A part of me… [insert an unwanted feeling].
- I am so deeply grateful *in* this moment for….
- I am so much more than what's happening around me.
- What's within me is greater than anything outside of me.
- I may be having this experience, but this experience doesn't have me.

I simply repeat these mantras over and over when I'm feeling triggered, scared, frustrated, upset, or having any other unwanted or low vibrational feeling. Although I didn't believe all of them at first, over time and after repeating them, they began to resonate with me. These statements help me recalibrate my energy and realign with my highest truth. Feel free to write any of these mantras in your journal to come back to later or come up with your own.

As we close this chapter on Metaphysics and Mental Science, let's take a moment to appreciate the vast landscape of our mind and the unseen forces guiding our journey. These principles and faculties, deeply rooted in the metaphysical realm, offer a map for navigating life's challenges and triumphs. By understanding and leveraging them, we not only enrich our personal experiences but also touch the lives of those around us. It's a dance between the tangible and intangible, the seen and the unseen, all woven together in the magnificent tapestry of existence. As you move forward, may you be inspired to delve deeper, question more, and find a harmonious balance between the knowledge of the world outside and the wisdom within.

We have only touched the very tip of the iceberg so far.

PART III

ACTION

"Act as if what you do makes a difference. It does."

— William James

Chapter 11

Be the BEST You

"Success is peace of mind which is a direct result of self-satisfaction in knowing you did your best to become the best you are capable of becoming."

— John Wooden

In Chapter 1, we discussed two major concepts under the third A of the Triple A's of Transformation: Action. The first concept was "Massive Imperfect Action," otherwise known as MIA. The second concept was understanding that action isn't about frantically doing but mindfully being.

It's time to begin using these concepts to change our reality. We will no longer talk about the actions we need to take—we will take them!

In the remaining chapters, I will be taking you through a process I normally take my Marriage Mindshift clients through. However, if you keep an open mind, you will realize this process works for any and all relationships. Because, as I mentioned, *everything* is a relationship.

The first phase of the Marriage Mindshift process is called "Be the BEST You." BEST is an acronym for Brilliant, Empowered, Successful, and Transcendent. Our first objective in any relationship transformation is to become the best version of ourselves. I also like to call it "cleaning up our side of the street." Once we clean up our part of the relationship mess we're in, we will finally be able to see what is ours and what is theirs.

Often, I find people who have been working on themselves through personal development, therapy, or other spiritual practices have worked through many of their personal demons. But what they haven't yet done is manifest their best self *in* their most intimate (or challenging) relationships.

So, let's begin exploring what action steps you can take to "Be the BEST You!"

STEP 1: TAKE RADICAL RESPONSIBILITY

I am 100 percent responsible for the results in my relationship.

In Chapter 3, we discussed understanding that our relationship is a perfect reflection of our beliefs. Another way to look at this is taking 100 percent responsibility for our relationship results. Remember the Law of Thinking? It states our results are ultimately caused by our beliefs. And, therefore, our relationship results are determined by the beliefs we hold about how we relate to the world around us.

I know this is a bold statement and many who have been through traumatic experiences in their relationships may want to disagree. But I'm not the first person to share this concept. Many therapists and thought leaders have introduced this belief before me. And it's not to blame or shame anyone—this powerful and life-changing belief is meant to empower and transform our lives and our world.

Let me put it this way: We may not be able to control a given situation outside ourselves or control what happens *to* us. But we can take radical responsibility for our *experience* of the event. Here is where our power lies. Here is our opportunity to change the stories that have held us back, that have kept us in victimhood. By taking full responsibility— remember our response-ability is our ability to respond—we can change our outcomes and transform our lives.

Once you've accepted the belief that we are 100 percent responsible for our experience, you will be able to take the next step.

STEP 2: TAKE PERSONAL INVENTORY

I am open and willing to take a personal inventory of my life in the interest of growth and transformation.

Napoleon Hill wrote, "Take inventory of yourself, see if any remnants of fear are standing in your way. Then you may grow.…" If growth is our objective, then we must take inventory of where we are to know where we need to grow.

This action step will help us identify the areas we still need to clean up in our relationship. It's time to take an honest look at ourselves.

One night, I had a horrible dream. I was in a dark room facing a mirror. I was scared to look at my reflection, fearing it wasn't pretty. When I finally mustered the courage to look myself in the eyes, I saw an awful figure resembling death. Her yellowish-red eyes pierced through the cracks of the crusty dark hair covering her face. She grinned at me with an evil smile, her teeth covered in a blackish ooze. This scary monster was me. I remember jumping awake, terrified because, for the first time in my life, the reflection in the mirror was exactly how I felt about myself.

Only a few months later, after doing much of the work I'm sharing with you, I had the exact same dream. This time, though, when I looked in the mirror, the once horrific reflection was gone. I was no longer a dark, scary, death-like monster. I was human. I could actually see and feel the love in my eyes. I had faced my greatest fear—me—and aligned with whom I want to be both inside and out.

ACTIVITY: TAKING PERSONAL INVENTORY

Let's pause here to take personal inventory in your relationships. If it helps, you can pick your most challenging relationship right now. Write down some things you know you can improve in the relationship—in what way can you show up better in this relationship?

For example, when I went through this process, I identified:

- My tone of voice can be very piercing and powerful.
- Words are my weapon of choice, and I can be a word ninja sometimes.
- I was allowing Denver's feelings to dictate mine— when he was upset, I got upset. When he was happy, I was happy.
- I was looking at Denver's actions or inaction to feel loved.
- I didn't trust myself with men.
- I didn't know how to be a good friend first and foremost.
- My go-to communication style was passive-aggressive (sarcastic).
- I isolated myself in my relationship and didn't give much attention to my other friendships.
- I had a victim mentality—I caught myself complaining about my husband to my friends and colleagues.
- I lacked gratitude, trust, and faith.

These were just a few of the things I could take responsibility for in my marriage. Now it's your turn. Write down the thoughts, feelings, actions, or beliefs you can take responsibility for in your relationship. Don't be hard on yourself if they don't all come to you at once. This is a process that will continue to unfold as you go.

Another way to take personal inventory is to use "The Flower of Life" in the following exercise.

ACTIVITY: THE FLOWER OF LIFE

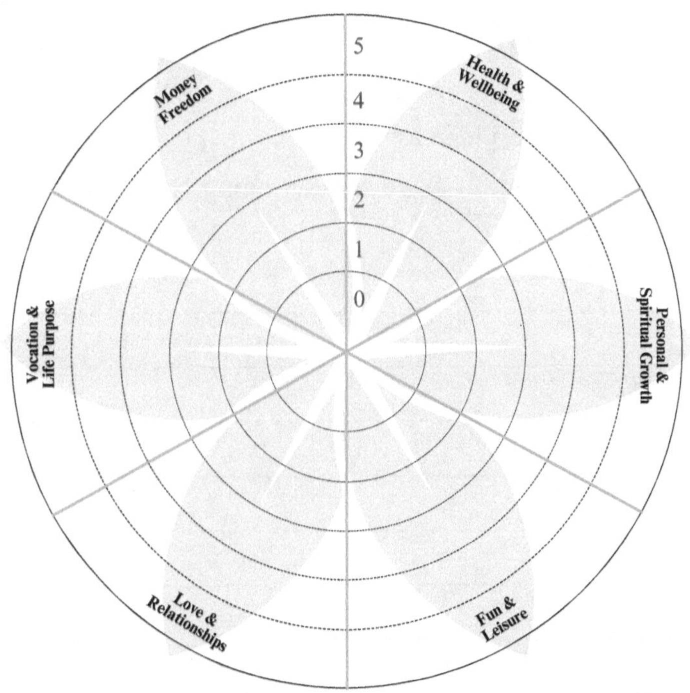

Take some time to complete this life assessment. The five bars in each category (petal) represent how fulfilled you feel in each area. Zero being completely unfulfilled and unsatisfied with your results in that area, and five being completely fulfilled and satisfied in that area. Color in or mark the appropriate number according to your current level of fulfillment in each area.

Using the Flower of Life self-assessment you just completed, journal about any longings or discontent you have in each of the areas with less than a five. You might be completely satisfied in certain areas right now, and that's great.

We know, as our journey continues, new longings and discontent will appear as life seeks to grow *through* us. Most of us will likely have some longings or discontent in every area of life.

____

____

____

____

____

____

____

Now let's take a closer look at your love and relationship petal of life. Inventory your most recent disagreement or argument in either your marriage or your most challenging relationship. Remember, every conflict is an opportunity for even more intimacy in your relationship.

What happened before, during, and after this challenge? Did you resolve it? If so, how did you do it? If not, what happened? Do you sweep things under the rug and pretend they didn't happen? Do you spend days ignoring each other, and once enough time passes, go back to being nice to one another? Does one person apologize first? Do you make time to talk things out? This is your opportunity to take inventory of your most challenging moments. I promise that within these moments are gems that can propel your relationship forward.

Another important part of taking inventory in your relationships is understanding your triggers. In Chapter 8, I shared my Inner Mosaic method to help you get to the root of your triggers and a deeper understanding of *why* you feel and act the way you do.

It's important to be aware of your triggers to find the best ways to support yourself in those moments. Our ultimate goal is to learn how to love and trust all parts of ourselves. To do that, we must understand what situations trigger our greatest fears.

ACTIVITY: IDENTIFYING YOUR TRIGGERS

Let's take another moment here to identify the triggers you *do* know about. As you continue to live by the Triple A's of Transformation, you will become aware of more. And remember, often your greatest triggers are attached to your deepest fears. They can also be associated with traumatic experiences. As I said, we call these pivotal moments memories that left an imprint on your life. Write down 5-10 of your biggest pet peeves about your partner or the relationship you are inventorying. Within these are your relationship triggers.

STEP 3: RECLAIM YOUR POWER

I can have an experience without that experience having me. I choose the meaning I give to circumstances in my life.

Once you understand what your triggers are, it's time to reclaim your power and release the hold these triggers have on you. Another way to put this is to neutralize your triggers; remove the emotional charge attached to specific situations.

In Chapters 8 and 9, we talked about the Inner Mosaic method and the art of forgiveness. Both these tools help you neutralize triggers and reclaim your power. Another very powerful technique is to rewrite the story you're telling yourself about your current situation. Often, we don't realize we have added a narrative (thoughts) to the facts of the situation and this narrative is causing our emotional triggers (feelings). Ultimately, we are in control of the meaning we give to people, places, and things.

As you build your mental muscles and practice using the Inner Mosaic method, you will understand *why* you're triggered by certain people, places, or things. This understanding will allow you to support the parts of you that have jumped into the driver seat of your bus. And once you can acknowledge who's driving, it's easier to support yourself through whatever situation you might be going through.

Right now, as I add my final thoughts and teachings to this book, so many things are happening. I have noticed I have an overwhelming feeling and frustration with the situation and the people around me. But I know it's not them, it's me.

As I reflect on the story I'm telling myself, I find it's a story about not feeling supported, having to do everything myself, and life never being easy for me. Do any of these stories or themes resonate with you? I'm sure at least one does.

When I think back to my earliest memory of feeling unsupported, having the weight of the world on my shoulders, and life not being easy, I'm taken back to my seven-year-old self.

Remember Sam Sam? Her theme or story is "Abandoned and Alone." Sam Sam lost her uncle Richard to a heart attack. This was her grandmother's friend who lived with them in a multi-generational home. Uncle Richard picked Sam Sam up from school every day. He was a second father to her because her father wasn't around after her parents' divorce. He was Sam Sam's best friend and spoiled her with toys and treats. After Uncle Richard passed, Sam Sam's life changed a lot. Her mom got remarried, they moved to a different town, and everything was in a constant state of change. Her father being absent and her uncle passing away suddenly led Sam Sam to create the story in her head that "men leave me."

Over the years, Sam Sam also carried a heavy story in her heart. She felt like her uncle's death was her fault. You see, the day before he passed, Uncle Richard told Sam Sam he wasn't feeling good but asked her not to tell anyone else in the family. That's exactly what she did. Later, she blamed and shamed herself for not speaking up because she thought maybe, just maybe, it could have saved her uncle's life. As an adult, I know the story I told myself as a child wasn't true, but it's not about it being true; it's about how real it felt and how much I believed it. This led the seven-year-old version of myself to feel the weight of the world, the heaviness of responsibility for someone's life (or death).

Isn't it amazing how deep we can get from simply feeling overwhelmed and frustrated? I just said my week was stressful. But once I took a deeper look at the emerging story, I identified the Inner Mosaic part of me driving the bus.

Now that I've identified the part of myself that's here, I can release the overwhelming feelings and frustration. I can acknowledge I am not responsible for everyone in my life, and my actions (or inaction) right now won't lead to anyone's passing. I see Sam Sam needs to be reminded of this and needs my help in asking for support from those around her.

Reclaiming your power isn't about getting into a power struggle with the different parts of yourself or even with other people. Reclaiming your power is about stepping into the truth of what's really going on and learning how to trust all parts of yourself to navigate through the tough times, no matter the circumstances.

ACTIVITY: RECLAIMING YOUR POWER

Take some time to recall an old memory of a challenging time in your life and identify some of the lessons you were able to learn from that experience. Once you've done that, take a moment to change the story you have once told yourself about that situation.

Maybe in the past you said you were bullied, scammed, or misguided. Whatever it may be, now is your opportunity to change your narrative around the situation. If you learned how to have a backbone and stand up for yourself from that experience, then you can change that victim story to one of gratitude that you grew from the situation and wouldn't be the person you are today without that event. Go ahead; change your story.

Once you have taken radical responsibility, inventoried your part in the problem, and reclaimed your power, you *are* being the BEST you! I know, I know you might be saying, "That's it? Three steps? That's all we need to do to be the best we can be?" The thing is, these are three steps you can take to continue to show up as the best version of yourself day-in and day-out, but ultimately, *you* are the only one who will know if you are truly showing up in your best light. Remember, being the BEST you isn't about being perfect. It's about giving yourself grace to be human, make mistakes, and be messy at times. Then turning around, owning it, and being willing to be even better the next time.

As we continue on this Marriage Mindshift journey, the next phase of the process is where the rubber meets the road and the true test of will begins.

Chapter 12

Navigating the Storm

"I am not afraid of storms,
for I am learning how to sail my ship."

— *Louisa May Alcott*

Everything always looks worse before it gets better. The key to transforming your relationship is to remain unaltered and stay the course. Don't allow the circumstances to distract you from creating the lasting change you've been longing for.

BOILING YOUR WATER

In Chapter 5, I shared a story about boiling water. We've come to the time in your journey where you're going to start seeing the waters of life begin to get a bit rough. In the relationships I've supported, this is the part of the journey where my client's partner begins *their* transformation in the relationship.

Remember the Law of Systems and how to create a lasting change? When you change one part of a system, the system by law must and will change or it will come to a natural completion. This is the time when

178

your steady growth and transformation will begin to influence your partners.

But it's also important to note here that this is the point where most people get discouraged and stop what they've been doing. I have seen many partners completely regress to their most toxic behaviors during this part of the process. And the reason is this: When you change one part of a system, the system itself wants to return to its homeostatic state. So it will do whatever is necessary to get back to the familiarity of the old patterns and way of operating.

Many people have tried to be the change agent in their relationships, but when their partner becomes more symptomatic or it feels like their challenges are getting worse, they give up prematurely. They revert back to old behaviors and relationship patterns before they can create the lasting change in their relationship.

As a Marriage Mindshift coach, supporting my clients through this part of the process is probably the most important aspect of my coaching and one of the main reasons people hire me. Think about it this way: Why do you hire a personal trainer when you could watch a bunch of workout videos to learn all the different exercises they teach you? You hire a coach to keep you accountable and help you see when you're drifting off course.

Ensuring you keep the heat on while trying to boil your water (aka transform your relationship) is the number-one reason people end up hiring a marriage coach. But here's the thing—you *can* do it yourself. It simply requires you to work your mental faculty of will to help command your mind to stay the course when everything else around you says you're going in the wrong direction. Using all the tools in this book can and will give you all you need to create a relationship you would love. But sometimes it's easier said than done.

Let me introduce you to my client, Aurora. She is a beautiful mom, wife, and daughter. She came to me completely heartbroken and distraught after finding out about her husband's online activity. Aurora's husband was looking at and interacting with other women online, and knowing this brought up all her insecurities, not only about her body, but also about her worth as a wife and mother.

Aurora and I worked through the tools and techniques discussed in this book, and the woman Aurora emerged as is almost unrecognizable from whom she was before. Aurora knew her insecurities were not her husband's responsibility—only she could build up her self-confidence and self-esteem. We identified the Inner Mosaic parts that took over her bus and took her down very dark rabbit holes, like asking her husband for details about the women he encountered so she could compare herself to them. By learning to trust and love all parts of herself, Aurora slowly but surely began to see a change in herself. She started acting differently in her marriage and was no longer afraid to speak up for herself.

Shifting her thoughts and feelings about herself and the situation was hard, but Aurora kept at it. Every week, we discussed her triggers and identified new ways to view the situation, giving her husband's actions and inaction new meaning. Over time, as Aurora's triggers lessened, her husband's began to increase. He became more volatile and defensive about the situation. He was no longer groveling and begging for her forgiveness. His frustration grew and he started having outbursts and breakdowns.

Here is where most people give up and when Aurora felt like things were going backward. But I reassured her, "This is what it looks like while it's all working out." So, week after week, she continued to do her own work and showed up as the best version of herself in her marriage. Although the best version of herself was sometimes messy and unskilled, she kept getting back up and giving herself grace.

Remember when I said boiling water takes patience? Patience is exactly what Aurora practiced. She practiced being patient with her husband's progress, patient with him not being able to answer all her questions, and patient with his defensiveness and inability to hear her side. She was patient until one day, although delayed, he became the loving, caring husband she had been asking for. He soon realized there were deeper issues, which caused him to look outside his marriage and begin his own healing journey with a therapist.

Now don't get me wrong; their marriage (like everyone else's) isn't perfect. But I share Aurora's story because it's everyone's story. It's easy to run away and call it quits when the going gets tough. But weathering the storm, knowing clearer skies were on the other side, led to such a rewarding experience for Aurora and her husband. I just chatted with Aurora today, and she is so proud of whom she's become through this process. And better yet, she is grateful for everything that has happened in her marriage, even the breach of trust and betrayal she felt! She is grateful because she acknowledges the situation was the catalyst for her to become the empowered mom, wife, and entrepreneur she is today.

YOUR HAPPINESS LIMIT

The next tool is one I learned about later in my journey, but it has been a game-changer for me and my marriage. In a nutshell, it's one of those things that happens to all of us. I had a typical experience with my husband, Denver. Okay, okay, it wasn't just one experience; it was many.

But what happened was simple—we had recently decided we were going to work things out. We were actually doing really well with communication, intimacy was back up, and we were having lots of fun. Then all of a sudden, a wave of anger and resentment would rush over my entire body when a pile of dirty laundry reminded me that he had said he would help me with it. Or I would get triggered by the overflowing trash he had promised to take out or the never-ending list of "things to do" he never thought about because he never helped me do them.

Are you catching where I'm going?

In the book *The Big Leap*, Gay Hendricks calls this the Upper Limit Problem or ULP. He explains we all have: "An inner thermostat setting that determines how much love, success, and creativity we allow ourselves to enjoy. When we exceed our inner thermostat setting, we will often do something to sabotage ourselves, causing us to drop back into the old, familiar zone where we feel secure."

Let me pause here to explain a bad situation only feels secure because we've been there before and we know what to expect.

Hendricks goes on to explain that much of this thermostatic setting gets programmed early in childhood. That's where the Inner Mosaic comes into play. These settings are based on the Inner Mosaic part that manifests at any given moment. Based on our experiences, we are conditioned to only expect so much good in life. Have you ever heard or had the thought, "This is too good to be true"?

That's the exact thought that ultimately leads to an Upper Limit Problem or what one of my private clients named her "Happiness Limit."

I think that term is quite accurate. It's the limit we subconsciously place on our happiness.

Something else I've learned along the way is our limit on happiness is normally directly correlated to our self-worth and self-esteem. If we don't believe we are worthy of happiness and love, our limit for happiness is quite low. Therefore, we self-sabotage much sooner to bring us back down to the familiar feeling of loss, disappointment, sadness, or even anger.

I have found that those who work on their self-worth, self-esteem, and self-love slowly but surely increase their happiness limit over time. And before they know it, they're enjoying success and abundance they never thought possible.

When you find yourself in yet another argument, conflict, or challenge, take a moment to think about what was happening right before the incident. Was your life actually going really well? Did something really good happen that you had never experienced before? What about fun? Were you having the most fun or feeling the most loved you've ever felt in your life? *If* your answer is *yes*, it's likely you were simply experiencing and bumping up against your happiness limit.

And in honor of one of my coaches, Kirsten Welles, we'll call this "the good news."

I know that's a hard pill to swallow when things feel like you're at ground zero again or you're on a never-ending carousel of heartbreak and frustration. But the reality is you've simply bumped up against the edge of the life you've known up until now.

When you reach the edge of something, do you say, "Oh, no, that's it; that's the end, so we better turn back," or "We made it! And look, there's more to explore. The journey has only just begun."?

If you prefer to stay in your comfort zone and go back the way you came, I don't think you're reading the right book. It's more likely you prefer the latter—you like to celebrate the progress you've made and are ready and willing to keep going. If that's you, then this truly is *the good news*.

ACTIVITY: RECOGNIZING YOUR HAPPINESS LIMIT

Take some time right now to identify the last three to five challenges you've faced in your relationship or life in general. Now think back to right before the challenge. What happened? Write that down too. Okay, now think forward. What did you learn from each of those challenges, and how did you grow?

Make sure you do this exercise. It's an important tool to use whenever you face any challenge. And once you become skilled at using this tool, you will be able to shift your mindset in the middle of your next challenge to see it as an opportunity for growth and traverse it with much more ease, grace, and flow.

Chapter 13

The Inner Mosaic Dance

"Love is a melting of two souls, fully accepting the dark and the light within each other, bound by the courage to grow through struggle into bliss."

— Jackson Kiddard

One question I am often asked is, "How can the Inner Mosaic method help my relationship?" Maybe you're asking this question yourself. Let me tell you about what I like to call the Inner Mosaic Dance. When two people come together in a relationship, no matter the nature of that relationship, they will inevitably dance. There will be a back and forth. Sometimes the dance will be positive, when done consciously. At other times, it can be painful. Sooner or later, someone in a relationship will be triggered by the other's words or actions. In many relationships—friendships, family, marriage—I have been triggered over and over again.

An Inner Mosaic part comes forward and jumps into the driver's seat. And when this happens for two people simultaneously, they begin the Inner Mosaic Dance.

Sometimes both parties are unaware of their Inner Mosaic parts, which tends to lead to conflict in a relationship. When one partner is working on their Inner Mosaic Map, it's still common for the couple to fight because the initial partner doesn't realize their partner's younger, less skilled Inner Mosaic part is in the driver's seat too.

Imagine two seven-year-olds having tantrums while trying to express their feelings in an unskilled way and feeling unloved and unheard by each other, someone they care about, someone who is supposed to care for them. Their response to the relationship conflict will vary depending on the memory of origin and imprint made on them.

When you find yourself in an Inner Mosaic Dance with someone you care about, or even someone you don't like, it's important to become aware of what's happening to both of you so you can pause the dance for a little bit and get your bearings.

Here are some tools I have used both personally and professionally to help couples who find themselves in an Inner Mosaic Dance:

HALT

Before we learn any communication tools, we need to set up the ground rules for when it's best to talk and when it's better to save it for another time.

HALT stands for Hungry, Angry, Lonely, or Tired. I first learned this acronym while I was working in the substance use field. It was helpful in teaching my clients who were struggling with impulse control to *stop*, even if it was just for a nano-second, to make an empowered and informed decision.

HALT is actually one of the main tools I use for myself. Whenever I feel conflict arising about another person, I ask myself these four things: Am I hungry? Am I angry? Do I feel lonely? Am I tired? If I answer yes to any of these questions, I know it means I should halt. And I mean literally stop and walk away from the situation.

This practice is much easier said than done, for sure—especially in the heat of the moment when you've already lost some of your cool.

In marriage counseling, I used to teach both partners about HALT. Now that I only work with one partner, I have my client go back to their spouse and teach them this acronym to use in their marriage. Sometimes my client or their spouse will use HALT as a tool to get out of a meaningful conversation, which is *not* how this tool is to be used. However, most of the time, both partners understand the value of finishing their conversation when they're less heated and calm.

Another way to use HALT is simply to call a timeout or hit the pause button. Basically, it's a mutual agreement you will walk away from the conversation until you have both cooled down. The key here is to make sure you agree *when* you will come back to talk before you step away. Otherwise, a never-ending HALT can be torture for someone who likes to talk through conflict, while the other partner is living in bliss, happily avoiding any further confrontation. That's not going to help the relationship at all. Used wisely, HALT can save you from many unhelpful conversations and damaging arguments.

CONSIDER LOVE

Another tool for when you and your partner are at odds is to ask: What would love do here? Ask yourself this question anytime you find you and your partner have begun an Inner Mosaic Dance. Often, when you are coming from a place of fear, frustration, or anger, it can be difficult to access the love you have for your partner. But asking yourself, "What would love do here?" externalizes the problem long enough to identify what love would possibly do in the situation.

While this is a more advanced question to ask yourself in the heat of the moment, practicing asking yourself this question even *after* you already had an argument will help you become better and better at using this technique *during* an argument. If you were reflecting on the conflict with your partner, you'd ask yourself, "What would love have done in this situation?" Asking yourself this reflective question lets you begin to see an alternative to the way you behaved in the situation.

Okay, I'm going to pause for a moment here because I know for a *fact* some will be asking themselves a very disempowering question right now: "Why do *I* have to do all the work? Why am *I* always responsible for being the bigger person?"

This is, in fact, an Inner Mosaic part talking, a younger version of yourself wanting to be taken care of. It's likely a part of you that has taken care of others your whole life. A part of you that's tired of putting everyone else first and not being taken care of in return.

And to answer the question, you don't have to do *all* the work. You just need to do *your* work if you want to feel better.

Our partners aren't responsible for "making us feel better," just like we aren't responsible for saving them. But after years and years of doing what we thought was "helping them," we are burnt out and throwing our hands in the air.

Know you aren't alone. I, too, have experienced this type of compassion fatigue. Some might even call it people pleasing or codependency. It really is exhausting to try to make everyone around you happy without first filling your own cup. That's why asking yourself, "What would love do here?" from an expansive place where all people involved are loved is key.

GENERATIVE GRATITUDE

Did you know there are different types of gratitude? One type is practiced commonly around the world. This form of gratitude is in response to good things. It's dependent on *if* and *when* something good happens to us or for us. We call this *conditional gratitude.*

The other type of gratitude is less often seen but much more powerful. This gratitude is generated *despite* the circumstances.

Let me share a story about a man named Viktor Frankl. Frankl stood in the void of a concentration camp, a place where hope should have died, but within him flickered an undying ember. It wasn't just survival Frankl clung to—it was gratitude. It wasn't the gratitude that comes with gifts, joy, and success, but the kind you muster from deep within when life gives you nothing but suffering. This was *generative gratitude*—the ability to generate a state of thankfulness from within, regardless of external circumstances.

Even when Frankl's wedding ring—a symbol of his identity and past life—was stolen from him, he found himself grateful. Grateful to be alive, to have a mind untouched by his captors, to have a spirit that soared beyond the barbed wire. He realized that while they could take everything from him, they couldn't take his ability to choose his response. In the starkest of conditions, he chose gratitude.

Frankl's brand of gratitude was potent. It didn't wait for a reason to emerge; it was generated, consciously and powerfully, in defiance of his surroundings. His realization was profound—conditional gratitude is fleeting and depends on our situation, but generative gratitude is something we create, a strength that can anchor us even in the stormiest seas.

The lesson Frankl imparts isn't just about the power of gratitude, but about our ability to create it. Generative gratitude is an act of rebellion against bitterness and despair. It's a statement that says, "I choose to find light, even if I'm surrounded by darkness." From Frankl's experience, we can learn that it's not about being thankful for suffering; it's about being thankful despite it.

ACTIVITY: GENERATING GRATITUDE

How can you cultivate this powerful state of being? Take a page from Frankl's book of life to generate gratitude in yours. Each morning, start by writing down three things you are grateful for, regardless of the challenges you face. And in moments of tension or conflict, before entering a difficult conversation or addressing a concern, pause and write down three more things you are grateful for about the person or situation you're about to confront.

Here's how you can begin this practice:
1. Find a quiet moment each morning to reflect on life.
2. Write down three things you are grateful for. They can be as simple as the warmth of the sun or as deep as the love of a family member.
3. Before engaging in any challenging interaction, take a moment to write down three things you appreciate about the other person, even if it's difficult to find at first.
4. Approach your conversations and your day with the mindset of generative gratitude.

Now take a moment to write down things you are grateful for *in* this moment. I challenge you to list at least 10-20 things.

By following this practice, you align yourself with Viktor Frankl's legacy. You choose to see beyond the immediate struggles and connect with something timeless and positive within. You generate gratitude, not because your circumstances demand it, but because you choose it. This is the true power of gratitude—it's an internal creation, one that can change not only your perspective but also the world around you.

Let's honor Frankl's memory by living out this principle. Begin today, and watch as the act of generating gratitude transforms your life, one morning and one conversation at a time.

CONTENT VS. PROCESS

In couples counseling, one of the first things I used to teach was the difference between *content* and *process* conversations. Most couples only think and talk about the content of the situation; seldom do they get to the process.

A content conversation is when two or more people are talking about the context of the situation, topic, etc. In other words, it's details and facts. This is where most couples get in trouble when communicating. They try to argue about the content. They try to prove their partner wrong by stating facts about the situation.

On the other hand, a process conversation is when you get to the root of what each person is *really* trying to say. Most of the time, a true process conversation sounds something like, "I don't feel loved. I feel like you don't care about me. I feel unheard and misunderstood." Can you see how this is a much different conversation than whether your partner took out the trash, washed the dishes, planned date night, or spent all day Sunday with friends despite you mentioning you were feeling lonely?

When you have a process conversation, you get to the deeper meaning of the situation. It's when you get to the deeper feelings that each partner is having about current circumstances. The coolest part is you can't argue about how someone else feels. It's their feelings. Their feelings are neither right nor wrong; they just are.

When you feel stuck in a conversation because you aren't seeing eye-to-eye with someone, try switching to a process conversation rather than talking about the content. You will likely form a deeper connection and level of understanding with one another.

But let me clarify that it's important to identify content (or the context or details) of the situation so you can work through it to get to the actual process (or feelings), so don't overlook that part of the process; just don't pitch a tent there.

For example, you're frustrated with your spouse about the way they handle certain situations. Let's pick a simple and very common situation with many relationships. You asked your spouse to take out the kitchen trash because trash day is tomorrow, you're in the middle of cooking, and it stinks. You ask them to take it out so you can cook without the smell of rotting trash. Your spouse hears you and says, "Okay," but doesn't do it. They're still sitting on the couch watching a show. Thirty minutes goes by, and you know for a fact there were at least two commercial breaks since you asked. This absolutely infuriates you because this isn't new. You've had this argument before and it's become a recurring issue.

Can you identify the content and process of this situation?

If you're married or have been in a long-term relationship, you can probably relate to this example in some way or another. Right? It might not be the trash for you; maybe it's about spending money, their "tone of voice," or how friendly they're with the opposite sex. The list can go on and on. Okay, so let's get back to the original example and take our time to break down the content and the process so you can better understand what I'm talking about.

The *content* is that the trash is full, you're busy cooking, and you asked your partner to take it out. The content is also the fact that your spouse is watching TV, thirty minutes passed since you asked, and they still didn't take out the trash.

The *process* on the other hand is a little deeper. It's possible that you are feel unimportant or at least not as important as the TV. It's also likely you feel unseen and unheard as well. Maybe you even feel overwhelmed and frustrated and like you're doing everything on your own. The story you're likely telling yourself is, "They always do this—they say okay but don't move a muscle until I start yelling." This also leads to another story: "My spouse/family doesn't listen to me until I raise my voice and they know I'm upset." This can lead to more and more stories such as: "People don't take me seriously when I'm nice, or I'm too nice to people, and then they take advantage of me or take me for granted." It could also lead to the story: "My spouse doesn't respect me because if they did, they'd do it right away. They would know I only asked because I needed help."

Can you see how the process is a much deeper rabbit hole than the content—how the stories you've been telling yourself for many years can all come to the surface with a simple situation such as taking out the trash?

Once you've identified the process, you can use the Inner Mosaic method to help you get unstuck and give voice to the part of yourself that's showing up in this situation.

In the example about taking out the trash, the conversation can deepen by saying, "I'm feeling frustrated and taken for granted in our relationship." This statement in a conversation will have a much different response from an accusation like, "You never do anything I tell you to do when I tell you to do it!"

___

ACTIVITY: DISCERNING BETWEEN A CONTENT AND A PROCESS CONVERSATION

Take a moment to review your last argument with your spouse, loved one, coworker, or boss. Were you having a content or process conversation? Were you talking about the details of the situation? Did you dig deeper to talk about how you felt about the situation?

If you felt stuck in your conversation or didn't feel like you could come to a resolution, I'm guessing you were likely talking about the details of what happened and your differences of opinion. Now is a great time to reflect back on the conversation and identify the story you were telling yourself and how you were feeling about the situation. Use the space below or take out your journal to write down your reflection.

THE TALE OF TWO BRAINS

In my master's program, one of my professors showed us a talk by Mark Gungor, whose lighthearted wisdom on the differences between male and female brains was nothing short of an epiphany. Although I was learning this information to help other couples in therapy, it hit home in so many ways!

Gungor spoke of the male and female brains with a humor that was as entertaining as it was relieving. He described men's minds as a series of boxes, each one holding a separate piece of their lives. They step into one box at a time and one box only. Women's brains, in contrast, are a bundle of wires, everything connected to everything, emotions and thoughts running on a never-ending loop.

When he talked about the "Nothing Box"—the space where men retreat to recharge, to think about, well, nothing—it was a revelation. It was a breakthrough for me. It was a humorous way of looking at those silent spaces in my husband's day I had filled with questions and concerns. I had mistaken his quiet for distance, his mental "down time" for disinterest. Understanding the Nothing Box helped me step back and perceive his need for this space not as a rejection of me, but as a natural retreat.

Before, I had often felt like a victim of miscommunication, a prisoner of unmet expectations.

But understanding the different ways we process our thoughts and emotions freed me from that. It was a humorous lesson, but underneath the laughter was a profound truth about acceptance and understanding.

Embracing Gungor's wisdom, I saw that my husband wasn't avoiding conversation or connection; he was simply in his Nothing Box, a concept I now appreciate rather than resent. As I moved through my emotions, this understanding brought us closer. We were no longer speaking different languages; we were simply using different dialects.

With this new awareness, I chose to see our interactions as a dance rather than a battle, a co-creation of our relationship with humor and grace. This isn't about blaming or carrying the weight of our differences—it's about acknowledging them, understanding them, and even laughing about them as we weave them into the greater pattern of our marriage.

Ultimately, you can use the Inner Mosaic method in many different ways in your relationships. However, to keep things simple, all you need to do is remember the Triple A's of Transformation: Awareness, Alignment, and Action.

Once you become *aware* of which Inner Mosaic part is driving your bus, and you recognize an Inner Mosaic part is also coming out to play in your partner, it's a great indicator that both of you could use some time to reset and re*align* yourselves to what you would love. Last, but certainly not least, it's important to *act* from an aligned place rather than allowing your Inner Mosaic part to try to handle things alone.

Otherwise, you could get stuck in an unwanted Inner Mosaic Dance with your partner. And as much as we might associate dancing with something positive, this Inner Mosaic Dance can be a painful experience when not done consciously or with skill. On the other hand, once you become aware of your tendencies with your partner, the Inner Mosaic Dance can be one of the most transformative experiences in your marriage.

Chapter 14

The Upward Spiral

"Life is a journey up a spiral staircase; as we grow older we cover the ground we have covered before, only higher up; as we look down the winding stair below us we measure our progress by the number of places where we were but no longer are. The journey is both repetitious and progressive; we go both round and upward."

— *William Butler Yeats*

Another tool that has helped me time and time again is what I call the "Upward Spiral." This concept has been taught by many thought leaders for decades.

When you think you're back at square one and an issue keeps recurring in your relationship, I want you to think of the Upward Spiral of Life. We live in a spiral universe; our DNA itself is a spiral, and if you are anything like me, you are constantly working on yourself, trying to be better.

For that reason, I know you aren't going backward. You're actually going forward. But because we live in a spiral universe, it feels like we always come back to the same or a similar problem. The reality is we have simply come full circle and are on the next rung up on the spiral of life.

CELEBRATING THE LITTLE STUFF

As William Butler Yeats wrote, life's a bit like walking up a spiral staircase. We're often so focused on reaching the top that we forget to appreciate the steps we take, especially the small ones. It's the coffee made just right, the bed made just so, or the way your partner remembers to charge your phone when you forget. It's in the subtleties of our everyday interactions that the most important aspects of our relationship exist.

Let's face it; we live in a world that shouts, "Go big or go home!" But I want to turn the volume down on that and whisper, "Celebrate the small, for it's the heartbeat of our lives." This truth is particularly true in our relationships. We're quick to point out a partner's shortcomings but slow to celebrate their quiet acts of love. This needs to change.

Why? Because the small stuff is the good stuff. It's the secret sauce, the cherry on top, the fine print in the contract of life that says, "Hey, there's joy to be found here!" When we make a habit of noticing and celebrating these moments, we don't just add a dash of joy to our day—we start a positive chain reaction in our relationships.

Imagine if every tiny act of kindness from your partner was met with the same enthusiasm as a grand romantic gesture. Think about it. Wouldn't that make you want to do more of those little things? That's the upward spiral in motion. It's about gathering all those bits of joy and letting them build on each other, creating an upward momentum that can carry both of you through life's inevitable tough times.

And let's be real—not every day can be fireworks and shooting stars. But can we find something to celebrate even on a Monday morning when the skies are gray and the toast is burnt? I believe we can—and we should. That's how we keep moving up the spiral of life.

ACTIVITY: WRITING DOWN YOUR WINS

Take a moment to write down as many small wins as you can think of in your relationship. What progress have you made in your relationship? What are you proud of in yourself today? What shifts have you already made?

____

____

____

____

____

____

____

So, as we move forward, let's remember to cheer for the small wins just as loudly as we do for the big ones because life, much like love, thrives on the little things. And who knows? By the time we reach the top of that staircase, we might just find those little moments that gave us the most joy and the most reason to celebrate.

REMEMBER HOW FAR YOU'VE COME

In the journey of life and love, we're always adding to our story, one page at a time. It's great to focus on the day-to-day narrative, celebrating those little wins I mentioned earlier. But there's something profoundly grounding about pausing, turning around, and casting a glance over the chapters you've already written together. It's about acknowledging not just the steps taken but the distance covered.

We often wait for anniversaries or significant events to reflect on our relationship's progress. However, the act of looking back shouldn't be reserved for special occasions. It's an everyday practice, a quiet meditation on the life you've built side by side. Think of it as stopping on that upward spiral staircase and looking down for just a moment—not with fear or dizziness, but with awe at the height you've reached through countless small ascents.

This retrospective view can be powerful. It's not merely a nostalgic trip down memory lane; it's an inventory of successes, a ledger of love's investments that have matured over time. When you take the time to remember the tough days you've weathered together, the small disagreements you've navigated, the personal triumphs, and the shared joys, you start to see the mosaic of your relationship. Each little win, each shard of shared happiness or challenge overcome, becomes a piece of the greater picture of your intertwined lives.

But why is this important? Because it offers perspective. In those moments when you feel like you're not moving fast enough or when doubt whispers you're not making progress, looking back can remind you just how far you've come. It reinforces your belief in the journey and in each other. It's fuel that can ignite hope during slow times and fan the flames of passion that may have dimmed.

Remembering how far you've come also serves as a compass. It helps you and your partner remember what you've been through and to realize you have what it takes to face future challenges. It reminds you that you've navigated and left behind every rough patch, and every joy is inscribed into the story of "us."

Emmy was, like me, married to her high school sweetheart and had two beautiful daughters. But when her husband left her to find happiness in another relationship, Emmy's trust was completely shattered. When her husband discovered happiness wasn't something he could find outside himself, he came back to Emmy, wanting to work things out. The betrayal Emmy felt cut deeply, but she still loved her husband and wanted to keep her family together. They found me, hoping I could help them through this difficult time.

The work Emmy did on herself and her marriage was incredible. She leaned in and worked to become her best self *in* her marriage. Feeling triggered daily, she continued to take radical responsibility for her relationship results and built a stronger relationship with all her Inner Mosaic parts. One of her biggest struggles was seeing the progress they were making each and every day. Their wins were small, but over time, they added up.

Emmy would call me frustrated and about to call it quits. When she did, we took time to look at how far she had come and how her changes had transformed her relationship. It was a beautiful reminder that even if our partners are unwilling to change at the moment, it's still possible to transform the relationship. Emmy is a change agent. All she did was focus on herself, and by continuing to take one baby step at a time, she was able to climb a mountain she never thought she could summit.

ACTIVITY: HONORING YOUR PROGRESS

Take time to journal about how far you've come. Describe what your relationship was like a year ago, or even ten years ago. Whether you made a conscious decision to transform your relationship back then or not, I know you can find something to celebrate.

And if you are struggling with finding the transformations or if you're just beginning your journey, take a moment to appreciate where you are right now.

Remember to take a moment now and then to turn around and look down that staircase. See the space once empty now filled with laughter, lessons, and love. Let the view from up high remind you every step counts, and every step is worth celebrating.

As we wrap up this reflection, let's prepare to walk forward again with a heart full of joy for the little things and a soul steeped in gratitude for our journey's length. And with each step upward, let's carry the comfort that comes from knowing just how far we've already come.

THE POWER OF VISION

As we stand on the precipice of possibility, the power of vision can transform the darkness in our relationships and our lives into a dawn of new potential. Earlier in our journey, we explored the "Flower of Life" exercise, examining the six essential petals that make up our fulfillment. If you discovered areas that scored less than a five, you tapped into your longing and discontent. That's your soul nudging you, whispering of growth and expansion.

Now, it's time to channel that longing into a vision transcending your current circumstances, to map out a journey toward a life brimming with satisfaction and joy. Imagine yourself as the architect of your destiny, drafting the blueprints of a future where each petal of your life's flower blooms in vibrant color.

In crafting your vision, I urge you to dwell in the realm of the present tense. Describe your life not as a distant dream, but as a current reality. Engage all your senses to bring this vision to life. Feel the vitality pulsing through you in your *Health and Wellbeing*. Hear the laughter and feel the warmth of connection in *Love and Relationships*. See yourself immersed in the activities that bring expansion in *Personal and Spiritual Growth*, and witness the fulfillment of your *Vocation and Life Purpose*. Smell the fragrance of success in your *Money Freedom* and taste the thrill of *Fun and Leisure* in your life.

Choose a timeframe that resonates with your belief and confidence in vision work. If you are new to visioning, or if faith seems a faint flicker, a three-year vision can offer the space needed for your dreams to seem attainable. If you're more experienced or confident, a one-year vision can act as a compelling catalyst for rapid transformation.

Remember, the dream you build must be worthy of you. It should elevate your existence, resonate with your deepest values, challenge you to stretch beyond your current self, require a touch of the divine, and ripple goodness into the lives of others. This is the five-point test of a dream's worthiness, as taught by Mary Morrissey, a mentor who illuminated the way for many.

As you write down your vision, apply this test:

1. Does it give you more life? Will this vision infuse more energy and vitality into your being?

2. Does it align with your core values? Is this vision a true reflection of who you are at your core and what you hold most dear?

3. Does it cause you to grow? Will the pursuit of this vision demand that you expand beyond your current boundaries?

4. Does it require help from a Higher Power? Is this vision grand enough that its fulfillment seems to call for a force beyond your own?

5. Does it have good in it for others? Will the realization of this vision contribute positively to those around you?

If your dream passes this test, it's not just a worthy goal—it's your vision, a beacon guiding you through the darkness and into the light of a life you would love.

Remember Emmy? When I first started working with her, I had her create a vision for the marriage she would love. One thing she and her husband dreamed of was traveling to Japan and having a beautiful family vacation during cherry blossom season. About one year after beginning their work with me, they did just that.

Emmy's dream materialized in the most beautiful way—it wasn't merely the long-awaited journey to Japan that thrilled her, but the profound transformation their marriage had undergone leading up to it. In the land of cherry blossoms, their relationship bloomed anew.

Emmy was wrapped in a newfound sense of love and support; she felt seen and heard in unfamiliar yet deeply comforting ways. Their communication had shifted, becoming more thoughtful and effective—not perfect, but an honest reflection of their growth. Just like the intricate patterns of a Japanese Zen garden, their interactions had come to represent a complexity that was both challenging and beautiful. This journey to Japan was more than a trip; it was a milestone marking how far they had come in their marriage by keeping their shared dreams at the heart of it.

ACTIVITY: CREATING YOUR VISION

Take time now to write out your vision. This is a very important step. Something I share with my clients all the time is a saying I've adapted as my own: "A sailor without a destination has no favorable winds." So, pick a destination and a direction to set your sails! Write out your vision for the life you would love. At the very least, make sure you have a vision for your relationship life petal.

____

____

____

____

____

____

____

Before we begin to wrap things up, I want to leave you with one more thought about your vision. Remember to hold your vision with an open hand. This means continue to use the mantra "This or something better still." Trust that the Universe, God, or whomever or whatever you subscribe to will bring your vision to you in the exact way you dreamed or even better. Whenever I feel like things aren't coming together the way I dreamed, I always remind myself, "This is what it looks like while it's all working out for mine and everyone else's highest good!"

As we close this chapter, keep your vision close to your heart. Let it be the lighthouse guiding you through stormy seas, the North Star in your night sky. Embrace the power of vision as both a tool and a talisman, a source of inspiration and a badge of courage. With it, you're not just moving forward; you're ascending toward the life you are meant to live—a life that's not only possible but is already waiting for you to claim it.

Chapter 15

And So the Journey Begins...

"It's not the destination, it's the journey."

— Ralph Waldo Emerson

In his book *The Hero's Journey*, mythologist Joseph Campbell talks about the moment when the hero "answers the call to adventure." Well, now it's your turn to answer the call. Simply because you are reading this book, I know something must be calling you to have more in your life and relationships. This is your opportunity not only to deepen your understanding of what's happening, but to do something about it.

You are the change agent in your relationships, whether you like it or not. But until you claim that within yourself, it's likely you will continue going through life as a victim of your circumstances.

Let's put these principles and the Inner Mosaic method to work in your life!

Going forward, you can use these tools to overcome whatever may be holding you back from success.

Remember: self-trust *is* the ultimate form of self-love. Many people teach the principles of self-love, but what I don't hear enough is the concept of self-trust. As I mentioned earlier, this is a multi-faceted concept. We have the "Higher Self" and the human self (made up of all our Inner Mosaic parts). When we don't trust all parts of ourselves, it causes trials and tribulations.

But when you choose to trust yourself, you open infinite possibilities. You are the creator of your destiny— your results are caused by your beliefs. So, choose to believe in *you*!

YOUR WORK IS NEVER DONE

One of my favorite personal development teachers is Stephen Covey. In his book, *The 7 Habits of Highly Effective People*, Covey shares the habit of "Sharpening the Saw." This concept showed me our work is never done. If we're still breathing, we always have something to work on, something or someone to forgive (including ourselves), and ways to grow.

So, as I send you on your way to put these principles into action, I want to give you some new saw-sharpening tools and helpful reminders.

THE CYCLE

Remember your journey goes through an inevitable cycle. I like to think of a caterpillar's metamorphosis. But, you see, the thing is that as soon as we think we have become a butterfly and our strain, struggle, and challenges are finally over, we go back to being a caterpillar.

Now, I'm not saying we go all the way back to the beginning. No, we can never unlearn what we have learned and never undo our growth. But we may often feel like we are back at square one; we are back in the chrysalis and feel like a globby goo of nothing all over again.

Metamorphosis happens over and over again in our lifetime. But it's important to remember our next level of transformation will always be preceded by what looks like a globby goo. When we feel discombobulated and discouraged, it's likely we're about to have yet another breakthrough.

I share the cycle as a tool because people might give up at the first sign of life going backward or feeling like they're failing. But I want *you* to be able to look the chaos straight in the face and call it what it is—just the cycle restarting again.

THE RHIZOME

The second and final lesson I want to leave you with to help you continue to sharpen your saw and keep moving forward is what I call the "Rhizome." Once at a business development retreat, I learned how bamboo grows. You see, certain types of bamboo have a unique way of growing.

One particular type of bamboo grows only one inch in the first year. In the second year, it grows to a whopping two inches. In the third year, the bamboo grows to an astonishing three inches tall. And in the fourth year, I think you can guess—yes, four inches. But in the fifth or sixth year, the bamboo grows much faster. It can grow up to six feet in that sixth year!

The question here is what causes the bamboo to grow so little in the first through fourth years and then exponentially increase in size in its fifth or sixth year?

Well, the answer lies in the rhizome layer of the plant. This type of bamboo, along with some other plants, grows beneath the surface first. It creates an intricate and massive root system beneath the ground in the first four years to stabilize the plant so it can withstand the massive growth in the fifth or sixth year.

Here's my point: Sometimes it feels like we aren't really growing or we aren't really making much progress. Some of my clients report feeling like they take two steps forward and one step back. It's exhausting to feel like you're making little progress in your marriage, family, community, and/or career. However, if you're really doing the work—I mean the deep spiritual, emotional, and mental work we have discussed throughout this book—and still don't feel you're making much progress, I know for a fact you're simply building your rhizome (your root system) to prepare for the massive growth you are about to experience.

So, don't give up too soon. Keep going and keep growing. You will never regret your growth and the person you've become in this process—regardless of the outcome.

Epilogue
Beyond the Brink

"In any given moment we have two options:
to step forward into growth or to step back into safety."

— Abraham Maslow

As I was finishing up this two-and-a-half-year process of putting my figurative pen to paper, something amazing happened in my marriage. The stories I shared with you throughout this book about my marriage happened almost seven years ago in the spring of 2016 to the end of 2018. It would be out of my character and a disservice to you if I didn't get you up to speed on what's been happening in my marriage now in 2023. I would love to say things have been smooth sailing and have only gotten better since my rude awakening, but that would be untrue.

The past year, from September 2022 to July 2023, has been quite a ride for my marriage. This wasn't another crisis; it was more like a checkpoint, a real gut check for us. It was about seeing how far I've come on my own journey and whether we could sync up our strides and keep climbing together. We had to shake things up, to break some old patterns that were holding us back. And let me tell you, it was intentional and necessary.

So here I am, getting real about the bumps in the road and how they're not setbacks but setups for something bigger and better. I'm not just talking about the tough times but also about the choices I made to face them head-on. It's about not settling for "good enough" and daring to dream of what our marriage could be. It's been a year of pushing boundaries and unlocking new levels of our relationship.

This is the story of how we didn't just go through it but grew through it. And I'm excited to take you through this chapter, where every twist and turn has led us to a higher place in our marriage.

THE HERE AND NOW OF US

Life these days is marked by a newfound sense of understanding and patience between Denver and me. It's like we've learned to stand with each other in the storm without trying to fix it all the time. That's a big leap from where we used to be, always trying to paddle out of rough waters.

These days, it's the little things that mean a lot. A text from Denver in the middle of a hectic day can be a real lifeline. And our home? It's become a reflection of us—less clutter, more peace. Every clean and organized corner feels like a victory.

We've both grown a lot. Denver's journey into self-improvement is remarkable. He's finding his own path, learning principles that, interestingly, align with the teachings in my book. It's not that he's following my guidance directly; he's making these discoveries on his own, which is incredibly important. It's affirming to see our individual growth paths converging into shared values and principles.

The girls are thriving, too. Witnessing the changes, they're learning about resilience and empathy as their world evolves. Denver's developing bond with them is something I've longed to see from the start. Their growing connection isn't just heartwarming; it fills me with an immense sense of joy and fulfillment. It's everything I ever hoped for—a deep, loving bond between them and their father, something that enriches our family life immeasurably.

Our past, with all its ups and downs, has turned into something we're actually thankful for. We've gotten better at dealing with the leftover challenges, handling them with more honesty and teamwork.

Looking ahead, we're excited about what's next. Exploring new places, building a life that really feels like ours, and even considering the idea of renewing our vows. It's about celebrating how far we've come and embracing the future with open arms.

So, yeah, the future looks pretty bright from where we're standing. We've become a solid team, best friends who are up for whatever life throws our way, knowing we'll handle it together.

THE JOURNEY BEHIND US: Navigating the Boiling Point

As I reflect on the recent chapter of our lives, I realize Denver's journey into his dark night actually began back in 2019, around the time I was fully stepping into my professional role as a therapist and developing my practice and coaching business. This was a period marked by his remarkable support for my ambitions, a time of collective optimism and growth.

The turning point came in August 2021, when we made the intuitive decision to sell our townhome, a process that culminated in January 2022 with the finalization of the sale. This decision, though rooted in a deep sense of timing and intuition, ushered in a series of unforeseen challenges. Moving in with family, initially a logical step for transition, began to magnify the latent tensions and unaddressed issues in our relationship. The constraints of our new living situation brought Denver's underlying restlessness and dissatisfaction to the fore, revealing a stark contrast to his earlier encouragement of my professional endeavors.

The supportive partner who had enthusiastically backed my business ventures was gradually overshadowed by someone wrestling with personal demons. As I delved deeper into my journey of growth, Denver's path diverged, leading him into a silent struggle characterized by addictive traits. This divergence in our journeys wasn't just about professional growth but also about how we each coped with life's stresses and changes.

A family gathering following his uncle's funeral in 2022 became a vivid symbol of the chasm that had developed between us. My decision to leave alone that night was not just an act of drawing boundaries; it was a declaration of my own identity and independence, a refusal to let Denver's choices dictate my emotional wellbeing.

Our ensuing discussions about the possibility of separation brought to the surface all the raw emotions and deep-seated doubts Denver harbored about our marriage. It was a time fraught with emotional upheaval, highlighting both his inner turmoil and the strains in our relationship.

After this incident, Denver moved out of my grandmother's house. This marked a period of difficult choices and profound changes. Setting firm boundaries was challenging because it often reinforced the narrative of me being the "bad guy" in his eyes, but it was crucial for our children's safety and a demonstration of healthy boundary-setting.

During this time, our daily communications dwindled, and we began the process of letting go. The distance between us grew, not just physically but emotionally. My frustration with Denver's poor decisions, coupled with his perception of my boundaries as controlling, eventually led us to a serious discussion about divorce. For him, it was about seeking freedom and space, while for me, it was about not allowing his downward spiral to affect our family.

The moment we started filling out the divorce papers was a sobering reality check. As we navigated through the process, it became painfully clear how deep Denver's struggles were. This, coupled with our enduring connection—highlighted by the remarkable shared dreams we had—led me to realize that finalizing our divorce at this point wasn't right. It was a poignant reminder of the complexity of our relationship and the unbreakable bond we still shared, despite the challenges we faced.

Even though we decided to halt the divorce proceedings, the journey wasn't smooth sailing. A pivotal moment came in February 2023, around my birthday. The tension was palpable as Denver chose a work party over celebrating with me, a decision that deeply hurt me. This was a turning point in addressing my codependent traits, highlighting the need to prioritize my own needs and wellbeing.

Slowly, Denver began to emerge from the fog of his struggles. He found gratitude for me and our daughters again and grew tired of the life he thought he wanted. And I finally released my attachment to Denver's feelings and also leaned back into the power of gratitude. We began spending time together as a family on weekends and started "dating" again as friends getting to know each other anew.

By spring 2023, we made the decision to rebuild our life together. We found the perfect home to grow in and blossom as a family, a place where we could continue rebuilding and waiting for our forever home.

Throughout this period, our individual paths intertwined—mine marked by professional and personal growth, and Denver's by a deep, introspective struggle. This journey has been integral to our story, reflecting the resilience of our bond and our ability to navigate the darkest of times together.

ASCENDING THE SPIRAL TOGETHER

Now as we look ahead, the future is bright with the endless possibilities that await us. We stand at the beginning of a new chapter, united and stronger, more connected than ever before.

I have complete confidence in the path ahead, no matter the challenges it might present. Our journey has taught me that the transformation of any relationship begins within oneself. Our story powerfully demonstrates how one person can initiate meaningful change and steer a relationship toward a more fulfilling direction.

I'm filled with a sense of confident anticipation for what lies ahead. We've established a new way of living that honors both our individual desires and our collective commitments as a family. Denver's commitment to therapy and our move into a new home symbolize our dedication to this new phase of our relationship.

We are actively building a relationship that's founded on honesty, respect, and a deep understanding of each other's growth. Our daughters are witnessing this evolution, and their joy and resilience remind us daily of the value of this journey.

The path of healing and growth continues to unfold before us, and we are walking it together, embracing the challenges and triumphs that lie ahead. This isn't about returning to what was; it's about forging something new and enduring.

We face the future with unwavering faith and the wisdom gained from our experiences. Ready to embrace life's uncertainties with the love that has sustained us, this is our life now—a true story of redemption, recovery, and the powerful bond of our family's love.

A Final Note

Your Mosaic, Your Masterpiece

"The privilege of a lifetime is to become who you truly are."

— Carl Jung

I want to thank you for reading this book, for trusting me on this journey. The more people understand how their Inner Mosaic is working in their life, the more they will unlock their greatest potential and be able to truly shine their light in the world.

And that's exactly what I want for *you*!

I know if you're anything like me or my clients over the years, you want to leave a legacy for your family. Not only that, you long for and feel a deep responsibility to break the toxic cycles that have been around for generations in your family or in our world in general.

To do that, you must first become *aware* of what those toxic cycles are, *align* with what you do want instead, and take *action* from an aligned place. Reading this book has been an incredible step in your journey to doing just that.

Here is your final assignment in this book: Take some time to journal about what you would love your legacy in your family, life, and the world to be. Really sit and think about what you would love to be known for, the changes you made, and the feelings you left behind in those you love most. *How will the world be different because you answered the call?*

Again, it's your time to act and be the change agent. There's no better time than *right now*. You were born to be an agent of change in your life, your family, your community, and the world. So, begin within, and let your light glow and grow.

And if you would love some support in this process (and to stop the lone wolf syndrome), you can contact me at Samantha@thegemms.com, and I will gladly share how I have helped others just like you create their own Inner Mosaic masterpiece!

Acknowledgments

To my husband, high school sweetheart, best friend, and soulmate, Denver Kaaua, you truly are my handsome albatross (now seahorse) aka mate for life. I am so deeply grateful for you. You have helped me grow in so many ways and have held space for me to become the woman, mom, and wife I am today. Whether you knew it or not, you have been my greatest teacher, challenging me to become my best self in every area of life.

To my oldest daughter, Leilani Kaaua, having you was the best decision of my life. If it weren't for you, this book wouldn't exist. Although I never encourage parents to stay together for their kids, I have to be honest that it was you who gave me the strength and courage to get through the hard times and face my greatest fears. I also want to acknowledge you for helping me come up with the name Inner Mosaic; we always have the best brainstorming sessions together. Keep shining your light bright. I love you so much.

To my middle daughter, Jazlyn Kaaua, you are the backbone of our family. You keep us all in line and organized. I love how you are so mindful of everyone around you and you make sure each person feels included. Thank you for being such a beacon of light, pursuing your passions wholeheartedly and wearing your heart on your sleeve. You helped me expand my heart and connect more to my own feelings. Love you, my little mini.

To my youngest daughter, Haizley Kaaua, I am in awe of your certainty, decisiveness, calm confidence, and the joy you bring to everyone's life around you. You have challenged me to be a better mom and person every step of the way. I love the time we spend together in the mornings as I tickle you awake to get ready for school. Thank you for being unapologetically your true authentic self in every situation and with every person you encounter. I love you, my little squishy.

To my mom, Sheilah Kagehiro, where do I even begin? So much of who I am is because of you. Thank you for teaching me to dream big, that anything is possible, and the power of my mind. I am so grateful for your help with my girls, for being there for me and Denver when times were really tough, and for loving me unconditionally.

To my dad, Paul Yamamoto, I know you don't think I remember, but thank you for all the letters you used to write me when I was a little girl. Although I never responded and wrote back to you, I cherished receiving those letters when they arrived. I also want to thank you for helping me and Denver purchase our first home and giving us a place to begin our journey together.

To my siblings, Shaylah and Zachary Kagehiro and Taylor and Courtney Yamamoto, thanks for making me a big sister. Shaylah and Zachary, I am so grateful for you both in so many ways—for being my annoying little siblings to being the best auntie and uncle to my girls. Taylor and Courtney, you were closer to Leilani than me in age, and I love that she grew up alongside both of you. I love you all so much.

To my bonus parents, Keith Kagehiro and Cassandra Yamamoto, thank you for loving and caring for me as your own and helping to shape me into the woman I am today.

To my grandmas, (the late) Toshie "Betty" Komesu and Thelma Yamamoto, thank you for teaching me to be a strong independent woman, to never let a man dictate my worth, and to put my family first. You both are my heroes.

To my (late) "hanai" uncle, Richard Tanaka, although you won't read this book on this physical plane, I know you're reading it from wherever you are. Thank you for being a second father to me, for showing me unconditional love and being my very first best friend. You have made an enormous impact on my life and my soul.

To my aunties and uncles, (late) Charlotte and Stephen Teranishi, Leila Kagami, Sidney and Kai Komesu, Burton and Sandy Komesu, Wayne and Reina Yamamoto, Cheryl Yamamoto and David Suzuki, Joann and Gordon Hino, thank you for always loving me unconditionally.

To my in-loves (in-laws), the Kaaua and Kashiwabara ohanas, thank you for supporting Denver and me through our ups and downs and welcoming me into your families.

To the rest of my amazing ohana, there are too many of you to name, but you know who you are. I love you so much. Thank you for loving me and supporting me in everything I do.

To my friends, Lauren Hamano and Courtney Hirayasu. Thank you for supporting me since Leilani was one-year-old. You both watched me live through the stories in this book. Thank you, Lauren, for being there at the ER with me when I got diagnosed with my heart condition—I'll never forget the memories we made that day. Thank you, Courtney, for always having my back and encouraging me to demand the best from the people around me. I am forever grateful for the both of you.

To my friends, Chasidy Wright and Amanda Kodama, you both have taught me so much about being a good friend, setting healthy boundaries, and unconditional love. Thank you, Chasidy, for always asking me the hard questions and being willing to talk through any miscommunication or hurt feelings between us. You showed me how to forgive and lean in when things get tough. Thank you, Amanda, for letting me be your big sister at times and "tell it to you straight" without your feelings getting hurt. You created a safe place for me to be my authentic (unfiltered) self and showed me that the people who truly matter can and will still love me.

To my friends, Edna Castillo, Lin Yuan-Su, Karie Cassell, and Tomomi Ito, thank you for allowing me to build my dreams alongside you. It has been such an honor to watch each of you blossom into the amazing beings you are. I am so blessed to have had your wise and neutral support when going through tough times with Denver.

To my amazing collaborative partners and co-creators of the Clarity Confidence Connection community and movement, Candace McKim and Ranchelle Van Bryce, thank you for allowing me to be a part of our magical trio. I am so grateful for your belief in me and for allowing me to let my genius shine in our group. You both have taught me so much about being a soul-preneur and being a badass boss lady. Our summits were my lifeline when I was going through the most recent evolution in my marriage.

To my Dream Builder Coach Sisters, Tanya Caba, Gordana Radić, Kathy Biggs, Mariell Waltner, Taly Silkman and Penelope Rosas, thank you for always cheering me on and being such a wonderful support system through the transformation of my business and life.

To my Brave Thinking Institute (BTI) friends, Ryan Harris, Benjamin Blackett, Maggie Everett, Adelina Tancioco, Beth Burkens, Sonia Ovenden, Edna Castillo, Lin Yuan-Su, Karie Cassell, Tomomi Ito, and so many more, I love you so much.

To my Abundance Accelerator Mastermind Group, Jack Canfield, Kathryn Trestain, Tomomi Ito, Sonia Ovenden, Darci Brown, Greg Smith, Kaleem Joy, Kathryn Conlen, Laura Peiffer, Sandra Estok, thank you for giving me permission to completely reorganize and rewrite my book.

To the Clarity Confidence Connection (CCC) Community Founding Members, Pati Hoyt, Stephanie Zenker, Susie Day, Benjamin Blackett, Sam Bell, Cindy Smith, Rose Barr, Dotty Scott, Laura Barker, Jade Fulton, Jackie Mott, Noelani Oliver, Christopher Chamberlin, thank you for believing in the mission and movement of CCC and for joining us when all we had was a vision and a promise.

To my Legendary family, David Bayer, Judy Herman, Olga Rines, Adam Blair, Michael Knouse, Scott Gibbs, Ranchelle Van Bryce, Candace McKim, Roya Sayadi, Andy Way, Rose Barr, Christopher Chamberlin, and so many more of you I wish I had space to name here, thank you for helping me flush out my programs and cheering me on in my business.

To my Business Network International (BNI) ohana, there are far too many of you to name individually here. Thank you for helping me turn my baby business idea into a six-figure business. I have learned so much from all of you on how to be a better networker.

To my Hawaii International Pageant family, Tiare Lando, Cheryl Ho, Ashley Colozi, Gina Ross, Kara England, Danielle Nordan, Kaylee Maluenda, and Kim Kealoha-Ho, thank you for giving me the opportunity to completely step out of my comfort zone. Through my pageant experience, I created my platform The GEMMS® with Samantha Kaaua.

To my Gym Mamas, Tracy Wong, Nicole "Nicci" Buschmann, Nicole Brooks, Carolina Gibson, and many more of you, thanks for being a breath of fresh air and bringing fun and laughter into my life. I am so grateful for each of you and your daughters being a part of mine and Jazlyn's life.

To my book coach, Patrick Snow, thank you for supporting me in getting my book published and helping me with my near-impossible timeline. I appreciate you believing in me.

To my book coach and team at LA Writing Coach, Ashley Mansour and Jessica Reino, thank you for teaching me how to write my book using your T.A.P. method.

To my amazing editors, Tyler Tichelaar and Larry Alexander from Superior Book Productions, thank you for helping me clean up my manuscript and bring my book to life. Special shout out to Tyler; your guidance has been such a blessing to me throughout this process and your suggestion to ask Denver to write the foreword really helped to bring the book home.

To my amazing graphic artist and friend, Carlos Acevedo, thank you for helping me create the amazing artwork for my cover.

To my book design team at Fusion Creative Works, led by Shiloh Schroeder, thank you for designing and formatting my hardcover book to get ready for print and distribution.

To Ryan Seidner from Baker & Taylor Publisher Services (BTPS) for helping me with my printing questions and my beautiful hardcover book.

To Aviva Publishing with a special shout out to Susan Friedmann. Thank you for helping me share my hardcover book with the world.

To Juliet Clark from Winsome Entertainment Group, LLC for helping me publish the softcover and e-book versions of my book. Thank you for being an amazing support in launching my book and meeting all of my crazy requests with so much grace and kindness. Your belief in me and my book helped me in moments of panic and frustration.

To my legal team at Legal Paar, led by Roya Sayadi, thank you for helping me register my trade names for The GEMMS®, Inner Mosaic® and Marriage Mindshift™.

To my Author Accelerator class of Spring 2022—Jennifer Keith, Veronica Carey, Andy Way, Jessica Singh, Morgan McIntyre, Katelyn Davis, Juan Dias Rivera, JoAnna McSpadden, Leslie Bost, Linda Daugherty and Vanessa Molina—it has been an honor to write alongside all of you. I'm so thrilled to see all your amazing books come to life.

To The Salvation Army Family Treatment Services—special shout out to Candace Pang, Erika Warner, Chasidy Wright, Amanda Kodama, Kate Kahoano, Shanna Hadar, Jennifer Cabe, Leona Kulesa, Rachel Savereux, Pattie Ludlow, and all the other staff members, thank you for supporting me in becoming a better mom, wife, and coach.

To the Brave Thinking Institute (BTI) and my amazing mentors Mary Morrissey, Kirsten Welles, Mat Boggs, John Boggs, and Katie Augustine, along with all the other faculty and staff who have guided me through growing my coaching business. Thank you for all the wisdom you've shared with me that has helped me find my voice and clarify my vision for the life I love and am living.

To the former Argosy University Marriage and Family Therapy master's program, led by Dr. James Siebert and

Joy Quick, thank you for mentoring me well beyond the completion of my master's degree. Thank you, James, for always believing in me and for shaking me out of my head right before my comprehensive exam. You were a huge reason I passed my exam that day. Thank you, Joy, for mentoring me in my post-graduate hours and helping me blossom as a clinician.

To my Argosy University cohort with a special shout out to Mike Youngling and Xander Burgess. You really supported me in making it through our master's program and I wouldn't have made it without you. Thank you!

To all of my Spiritual Mentors with a special shout out to Cal. Thank you for seeing something in me that I couldn't see in myself. Your belief in me helped me to move out of the darkness I was in and learn to live from love with all of my being. I have so much gratitude for you in how you've mentored me and Leilani in remembering our Spiritual Truth. Another shout out to Kristi Stoll of Ancient Hawaiian Healings for helping me tap into my true power and build my confidence to support my daughters throughout their own spiritual journeys. I also want to thank Chikako Hoshino Powers for supporting me during our last rung up the spiral. You really helped me remember to slow down and be patient with the process.

To my amazing clients, although I cannot name you here, you certainly know who you are. I hope you know how much you are a part of this book and the Inner Mosaic method. You have helped me to finetune and reform my work to what it has become today.

You, the reader, thank you for taking the time to read my book. There are so many books out there and you chose to read this one. May the teachings in this book help you to find the beauty in your broken pieces.

About the Author

SAMANTHA KAAUA is a professional keynote speaker, author, and esteemed marriage coach recognized for her counter-culture approach to transforming relationships. As the founder of The GEMMS® with Samantha Kaaua and the creator of the Inner Mosaic® method, she is a beacon for individuals yearning to break through negative family patterns and lay the foundations for loving and trusting relationships.

Samantha's influential work has been showcased on major media outlets, including FOX, NBC, and CBS, and in numerous international publications. With a track record of helping hundreds enhance their relationships, Samantha extends her influence through the global Clarity Confidence Connection Summit, which she co-created and co-hosts. This platform empowers women to conquer obstacles and realize their potential. Samantha is dedicated to sharing her comprehensive understanding of relationship dynamics, offering a wealth of knowledge and strategies in her newest book *Finding Beauty in Your Broken Pieces: The Art and Science of Transforming Any Relationship.*

A lifelong learner with a profound interest in metaphysical, mindset, and spiritual literature, Samantha continuously cultivates her knowledge to enhance her coaching practice. Her unwavering commitment to personal and relational development shines through her teachings as she helps others embrace the power of self-love and self-trust. When Samantha isn't busy helping others transform their relationships and lives, she enjoys spending time with her supportive husband Denver and her three amazing daughters Leilani, Jazlyn, and Haizley. If they aren't globetrotting and exploring new destinations, they're cherishing their time spent hiking, jet skiing, and swimming in the natural splendor of their home on Oahu, Hawaii.

Samantha is on a mission to help save 10 million marriages by transcending the culture of healthy relationships around the globe. Her signature Inner Mosaic method, coupled with her metamorphic Marriage Mindshift process, stand as pillars of hope and transformation for all who seek to find the beauty in their broken pieces and the gifts in each meaningful moment shared.

About Marriage Mindshift Coaching

Embark on a transformative journey with Samantha Kaaua, a trailblazer in the realm of relationship coaching. Her innovative Marriage Mindshift coaching challenges the conventional approach to couples' therapy. Samantha has revealed a vital truth: Profound change can be initiated by just one person—you, the change agent.

A Marriage Mindshift is a profound, structural reimagining of your partnership. Samantha delves deep into the subconscious blueprints that silently influence your relationship, helping rebuild them with deliberate intention and insight. Her coaching underscores the power of individual transformation to create collective joy, demonstrating how a shift in your personal narrative can revolutionize the entire story of your marriage.

Designed for those grappling with the shadows of betrayal, such as infidelity or addiction, Samantha's coaching offers a roadmap to recovery when personal efforts seem insufficient. Her expertise is a lifeline for those ensnared in toxic relationship patterns, providing solutions when a partner's change appears out of reach. When traditional marriage counseling has fallen short, she steps in as the last beacon of hope, guiding you through a journey of renewal and resilience.

If you're ready to reimagine your relationship and take the first step toward a more fulfilling marital journey, connect with Samantha Kaaua today.

REACH OUT TO SAMANTHA:
www.MarriageMindshift.com
samantha@thegemms.com
(808) 444-4867
Or schedule a free Marriage Mindshift consultation by scanning the QR code below:

Don't wait for change—be the change. Book your session and turn the page to a new chapter in your marriage.

About Becoming a Certified Inner Mosaic Coach

Unlock the transformative power of the Inner Mosaic method and embark on a journey to becoming a Certified Inner Mosaic Coach. This certification is an invitation to professionals in the coaching and therapeutic fields, as well as individuals seeking a profound understanding of a model that integrates the complexities of human behavior with the grace of personal acceptance and growth.

Inner Mosaic is a revolutionary approach developed by Samantha Kaaua, inspired by the rich tapestry of systemic therapeutic models, including Bowenian, Attachment, and Internal Family Systems to name a few, yet transcending them with a unique perspective that honors the dynamic and multifaceted nature of the self. At its core, Inner Mosaic is about recognizing and loving all aspects of oneself to fully harness the power of one's entire being, forming the bedrock for all healthy relationships.

The year-long Certified Inner Mosaic Coach program is an engaging practicum that guides you through the intricacies of this innovative method. Through immersive study and hands-on application, you will learn to help clients navigate their internal landscapes with empathy and skill, enabling them to build a foundation of self-trust essential for relationship transformation.

This certification isn't just about learning a new coaching technique; it's about becoming a part of a movement that sees beyond the limitations of past traumas and labels. It's about stepping into a role where you facilitate deep, meaningful change in others by empowering them to integrate all parts of their being into a harmonious whole.

By becoming a Certified Inner Mosaic Coach, you join a community of professionals committed to a higher standard of practice, one grounded in compassion, innovation, and a profound understanding of the human spirit.

Embrace the opportunity to transform lives with the power of Inner Mosaic. Begin your journey today.

JOIN THE CERTIFIED INNER MOSAIC COACH PROGRAM:

www.InnerMosaicCoach.com

samantha@thegemms.com

(808) 444-4867

Or simply scan the QR code below to apply for the next cohort:

Advance your career, expand your expertise, and become a beacon of holistic transformation. Apply to become a Certified Inner Mosaic Coach today.

Book Samantha Kaaua
to Speak at Your Next Event

Bring the transformative energy and wisdom of Samantha Kaaua to your next conference, workshop, corporate event, or summit. Samantha Kaaua, a counter-culture relationship coach and an eloquent speaker, delivers engaging, thought-provoking, and inspiring talks that resonate with audiences from all walks of life.

As the creator of the Inner Mosaic method and a celebrated Marriage Mindshift coach, Samantha has dedicated her life to unlocking the potential within relationships and guiding individuals to a place of profound self-trust and connection. Her talks are infused with insights from her extensive background in substance use counseling and marriage and family therapy, delivering not just a message, but a memorable experience that can spark change in the lives of her listeners.

Samantha's speaking engagements are more than presentations; they're interactive journeys. She combines the art of storytelling with actionable strategies, leading her audience through the delicate intricacies of human relationships with grace and authority. Her keynotes cover a range of topics, including:

- **The Art of Relationship Transformation:** Learn to navigate the challenges of betrayal, toxic patterns, and stagnant emotional connections to rediscover the spark that ignites successful relationships.
- **Discovering Your Inner Mosaic Masterpiece:** Explore the power of embracing every part of your being to build stronger, more resilient personal and professional relationships.
- **Marriage Mindshifts Create Marriage Miracles:** Discover the counter-culture approach that's reshaping how couples connect and thrive in their marriages, even when conventional therapy has not sufficed.
- **Unlocking Your Greatest Potential:** Learn how to tap into your point of power, access your zone of genius, and receive all the gifts Life has to offer with more ease, joy, and flow.

Samantha is known for her captivating presence, leaving audiences empowered and eager to embark on their journeys of personal and relational growth. Her talks and workshops are a blend of profound truths, real-world examples, and practical advice, making complex concepts accessible and actionable.

Whether addressing an intimate group or a large assembly, Samantha tailors her talks to meet the specific needs and interests of your audience. With her dynamic approach and authentic passion, she creates an atmosphere of motivation and transformation.

Booking Samantha for your event isn't just about filling a speaker slot; it's about creating a milestone moment for your audience—a moment that will be remembered as the turning point toward deeper, more meaningful lives and relationships.

If you're ready to inspire and elevate your audience with a message that's both healing and revolutionary, book Samantha Kaaua to speak at your event today. Let her lead the way to a future where every relationship can become a masterpiece of connection and understanding.

CONNECT WITH SAMANTHA:
www.thegemms.com
Samantha@thegemms.com
(808) 444-4867

Book Samantha now and set the stage for an unforgettable event!

9 798888 964378